PUMP OPERATOR CUM MECHANIC MCQ

OBJECTIVE QUESTION ANSWERS

MANOJ DOLE

Digitization is the need of the time. In the future, training in industrial training institutes will need to be conducted using online internet to make training more convenient and easy. E-books containing a set of MCQ questions will be made available to the trainees as they need to be more accustomed to the multiple choice questions MCQ to prepare for the online exams taking place in their industrial training institutes.

With all these factors in mind, Mr. Manoj Madhukar Dole Instructor, Industrial Training Institute, Satara, has written books according to the new annual system and NSQF-5 syllabus. And they've created theoretical mobile apps and blogs to make training easier, and made all these educational materials available for download on the world famous websites Google Play Store, Amazon and Apple Book Store.

The books were published by Hon'ble Joint Director Shri Rajendra Ghume Saheb Regional Office of Vocational Education and Training, Pune on 9/1/2019, at this time Shri Prakash Saigavkar Saheb Principal Government Industrial Training Institute Aundh Pune, Shri Tukaram Misal Saheb Principal Govt. Q. Sanstha Satara, Shri Sachin Dhumal Saheb District Vocational Education and Training Officer Satara, Shri Yatin Pargaonkar Saheb Principal Govt. Q. Sanstha Kolhapur, Shri Vikas Teke Saheb Inspector Vocational Education and Training Regional Office Pune, Palekar Foods Products Pvt. Ltd. Entrepreneurial Chairman of Satara Mr. Nilkanthrao Palekar Saheb, Chairman of Hira Foods Mr. Ibrahim Baba Tamboli Saheb, Mrs. Shalmali Pawar Headmaster Government Technical School Center Satara and other dignitaries were present on the occasion.

Contents

Prologue

Pump Operator cum Mechanic MCQ is a simple Book for ITI & Engineering Course Pump Operator cum Mechanic, Revised NSQF Syllabus, It contains objective questions with underlined & bold correct answers MCQ covering all topics including all about the latest & Important about basic fitting operations in the work shop; use different types of tools and work shop equipment in workshop; perform precision measurements on the components and compare parameters with specifications used in work shop practices. He/ she is able to use different type of fastening and locking devices in a in Diesel Engine; cutting tools in the work shop following safety precautions while grinding; perform basic fitting operations used in the work shop practices and inspection of dimensions; produce sheet metal components using various sheet metal operations; perform basic electrical testing in a in Diesel Engine; perform battery testing and charging operations; construct basic electronic circuits and testing; manufacture components with different types of welding processes in the given job and inspect component using Nondestructive testing methods. During the later phase the trainee is familiarized with the identification of hydraulic and pneumatic components in a Diesel Engine Pump. He/she is able to identify and check functionality of stationary Diesel Engine - components, & engine performance on load and engine speed; diagnose and troubleshoot Diesel Engines for mechanical &electrical causes; servicing of plain/journal bearings, anti-friction bearings; identify and check functionality of major components and assemblies of reciprocating pumps, rotary pumps. They are trained to ascertain and select measuring instrument and measure dimension of components and evaluate for accuracy; use different types of conventional and special tools, hardware, fasteners and work shop equipment in the workshop; trouble shooting of pumps; identify and check functionality of major components and assemblies of centrifugal pumps; identify and check functionality of major components and assemblies of submersible pumps; carryout repairs in the fuel feed system; apply safe working practices and environment regulation in an workshop; construct electrical circuits and test its parameters by using electrical measuring instruments and lots more.

We add new question answers with each new version. Please email us in case of any errors/omissions. This is arguably the largest and best e-Book for All engineering multiple choice questions and answers.

As a student you can use it for your exam prep. This e-Book is also useful for professors to refresh material.

Foreword

Vocational education and training is imparted through the Department of Vocational Education and Training through the Department of Business Education and Business Practical to supply multi-skilled artisans in line with the rapidly growing demand in the industrial sector in the 21st century. All the occupations within the institutions are important, as the trainees from these occupations develop multi-skills as per the demands of the industry.

with the noble intention of making available MCQ e-books suitable for all businesses, considering that all the examinations in all the industries in the industrial sector are conducted online and include MCQ method questions. Mr. Manoj Madhukar Dole has written a very good e-book on MCQ method as per the new annual syllabus. This e-book will definitely be a guide for all the trainees, trainee candidates, training instructors and others concerned.

The author of the book is Mr. Manoj Madhukar Dole, Instructor Gov. ITI Satara has 17 years of training experience. Written as a new annual pattern, this e-book incorporates modern digital QR Code technology to understand the layout, simple language, and simple syntax, diagrams and videos for each subject. So I am sure that this e-book will definitely be useful for in-depth study and exam practice. The work they have done is certainly commendable.

Mr. Tukaram Misal
Principal Government Industrial Training Institute Satara.

Preface

DGET New Delhi and CSTARI Kolkata have been implementing an annual pattern for all businesses in ITI since the August 2018 session. The examination system will also be changed and it will be online from this year and since all the questions are of Objective Type (MCQ), the trainees are in dire need of in-depth study. It is with this in mind that we are delighted to present the books based on the old NIMI pattern and a complete overview of the new annual pattern, and we hope that these books will be a guide for all business directors and trainees. Is.

For writing these books, Johar Awate Saheb, Principal of ITI Akluj. Former Principal of ITI Satara Saigavkar Saheb, Assistant Director Shri Chandrakant Dhekne Saheb Regional Office of Vocational Education and Training, Pune, District Vocational Education and Training Officer Sachin Dhumal Saheb and Headmaster Government Technical School Kendra Shalmali Pawar Madam and son Adhiraj Dole, mother Kusum Dole, I am very grateful to my father Madhukar Dole and wife Ashwini Dole for their special guidance and cooperation from time to time.

Also, in a very short period of time, the book was reviewed by Shri Rajendra Ghume Saheb, Joint Director, Vocational Education and Training Regional Office, Pune, for his invaluable time in publishing the book. I am sincerely grateful for their feedback.

I am grateful to the Instructor of ITI Satara for there continuous support from the very beginning of writing the book.

From this book, I consider myself blessed to have shared my thoughts on e-learning with you. I will not claim that this book is perfect, because considering the perfection, this book is an attempt and is in its infancy. They will be valuable for improvement if they are tested and suggested.

Manoj Dole
Dated 9/1/2019

Acknowledgements

The industrial training and theoretical examination system of our industrial training institutes and these changes have been accepted by the craft instructors and the trainees. Theoretical examinations conducted in your industrial training institutes are also conducted online. Since these examinations are of multiple choice MCQ method, the trainees will need to get more practice of such questions.

With all these considerations in mind, Mr. Manoj Madhukar, Director, Dole Crafts, Katari Industrial Training Institute, Satara, has done a thorough study and with his diligent work and added his keen intellect, according to the new annual system and NSQF-5 syllabus, e-book of Katari and other machine trades. -Book) and they have created mobile apps and blogs on theoretical topics to make training easier and have made all these educational materials available for download on the world famous websites Google Play Store, Amazon and Apple Book Store. Training has been made easier by creating a print version and using advanced techniques like QR Code.

All these educational materials will definitely be a guide for all the trainees for in-depth study and for the craft instructors and other concerned who are imparting vocational training.

CHAPTER ONE

Pump Operator cum Mechanic QR Code Images

Download App
Online Test Exam
ITI Books
AutoCAD CAM
JOB & Apprentice
Online Theory
Computer Course
Trading Course
CNC Course
MSCIT Course
Shopping Business
Internet Business
Web Designing
Online Services
Top Sportsmans
Indian Army
Freedom Fighters
Top Scientists
Social Reformers
Motivational Speaker
Top Richest People
Join WhatsApp Group
Join Facebook Group
Like Facebook Page
PAN / Adhar / Licence
Passport

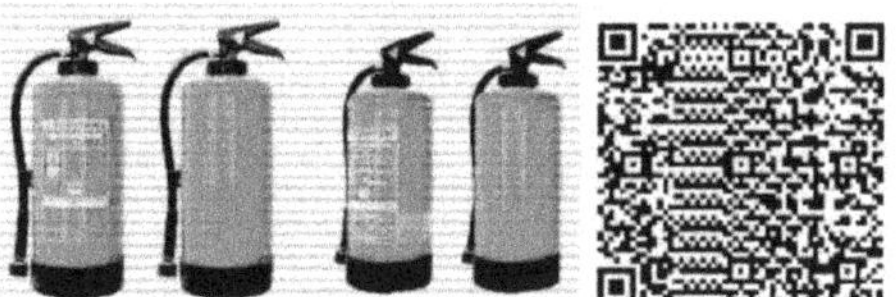

Fire extinguisher

Calliper

Hacksaw frame

Universal surface guage

Hammer

Centre punch

Bench vice

Files

Scraper

Surface Plate

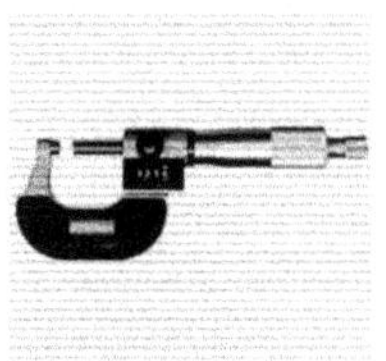

Outside Micrometer

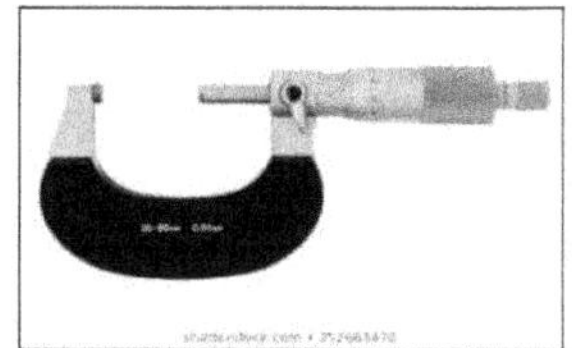

Micrometer

Depth micrometer

Vernier Calliper

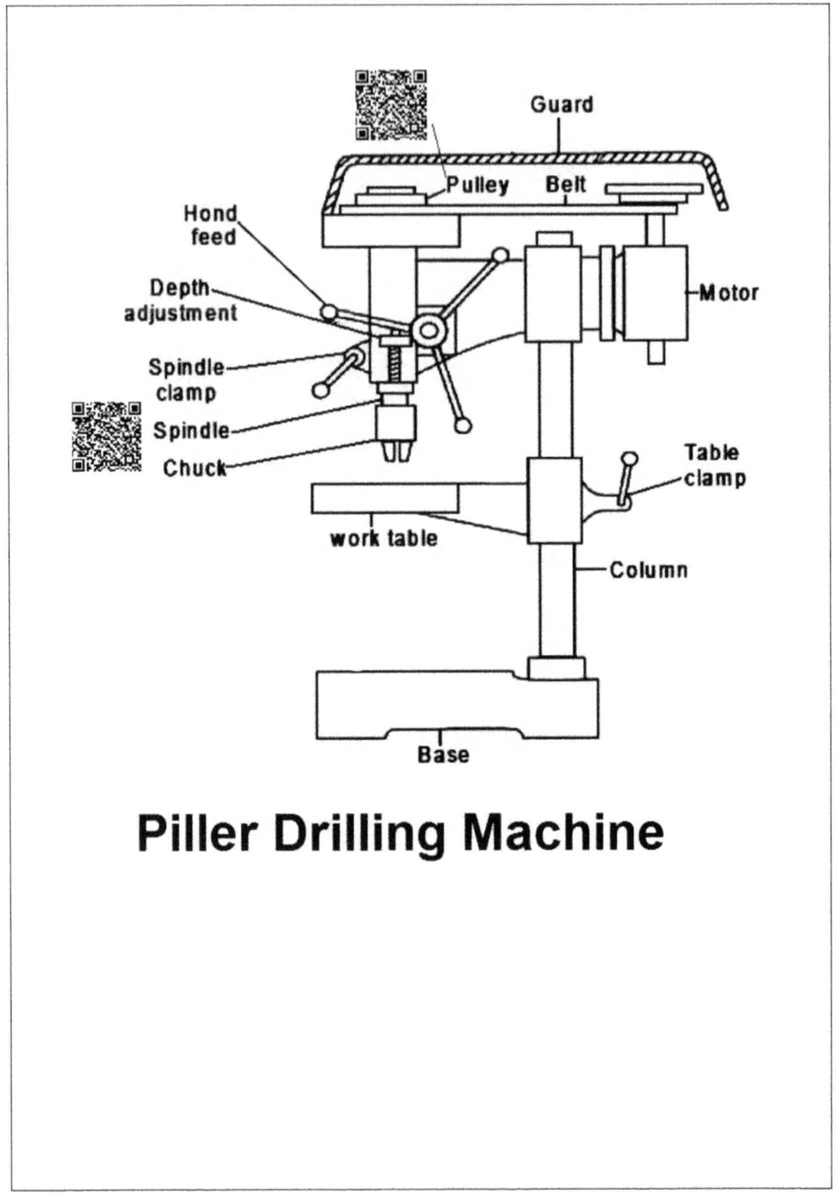

Piller Drilling Machine

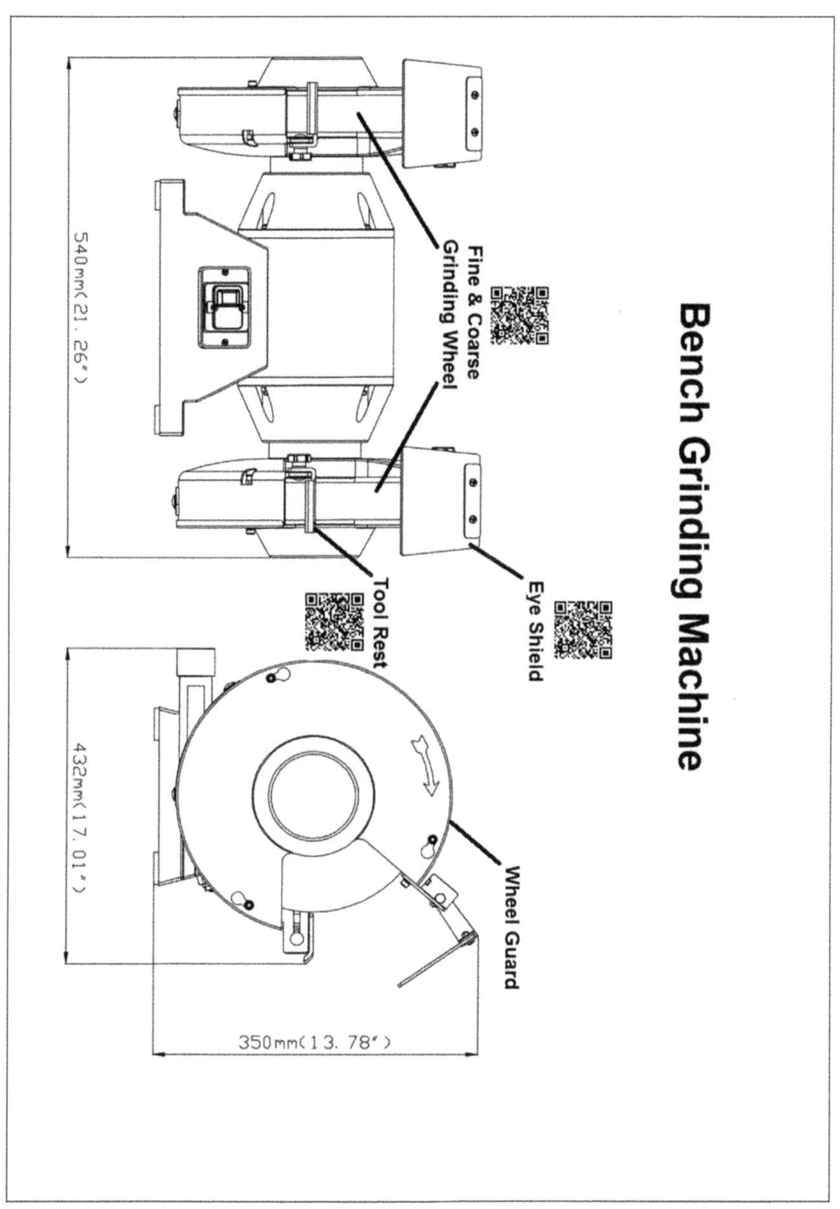
Bench Grinding Machine
Fine & Coarse
Grinding Wheel
Eye Shield
Tool Rest
Wheel Guard
540mm(21.26")
432mm(17.01")
350mm(13.78")

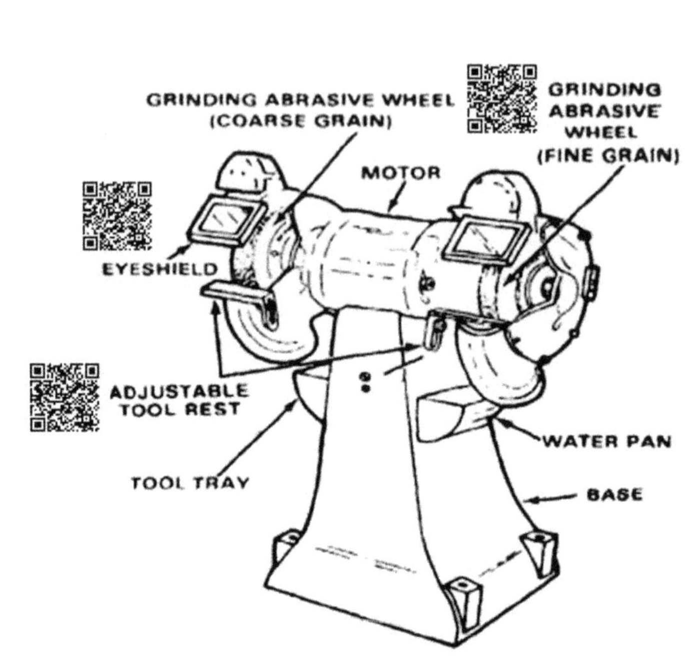

Pedastal Grinding Machine

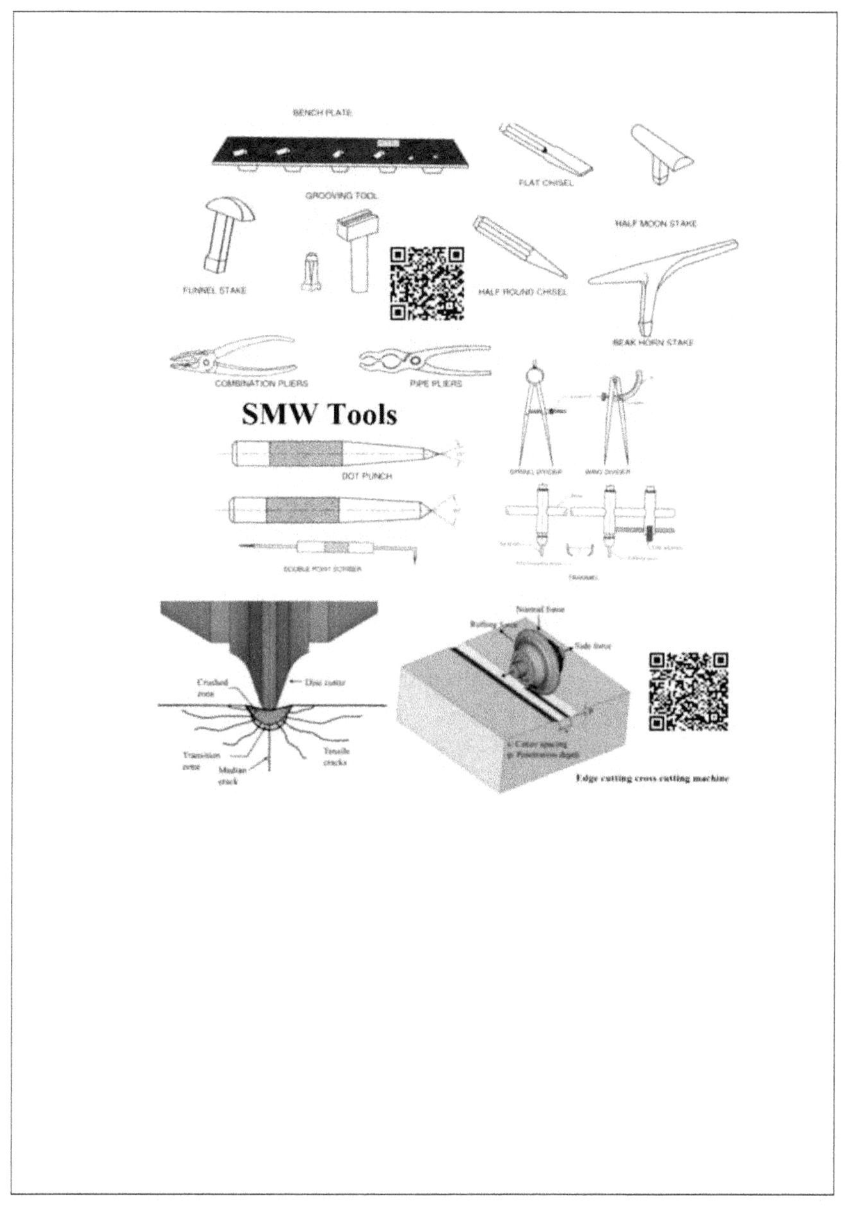
BENCH PLATE
FLAT CHISEL
GROOVING TOOL
HALF MOON STAKE
FUNNEL STAKE
HALF ROUND CHISEL
BEAK HORN STAKE
COMBINATION PLIERS
PIPE PLIERS
SMW Tools
DOT PUNCH
DOUBLE POINT SCRIBER
Normal force
Rolling force
Side force
Crushed zone
Disc cutter
Transition zone
Median crack
Tensile cracks
Edge cutting cross cutting machine

14 ITI Book MCQ - Manoj Dole
www.itibook.com
battery
capacitor
cell
dynamometer
electromagnet
heater
inductance
magnet
www.itigov.blogspot.com www.jobapprentices.blogspot.com www.ititests.blogspot.com
www.itibook.com

15 ITI Book MCQ - Manoj Dole
www.itibook.com
megger
motor
multimeter
ohmmeter
resistores
star connected alternator
voltmeter ammeter
wattmeter
www.itigov.blogspot.com www.jobapprentices.blogspot.com www.ititests.blogspot.com
www.itibook.com

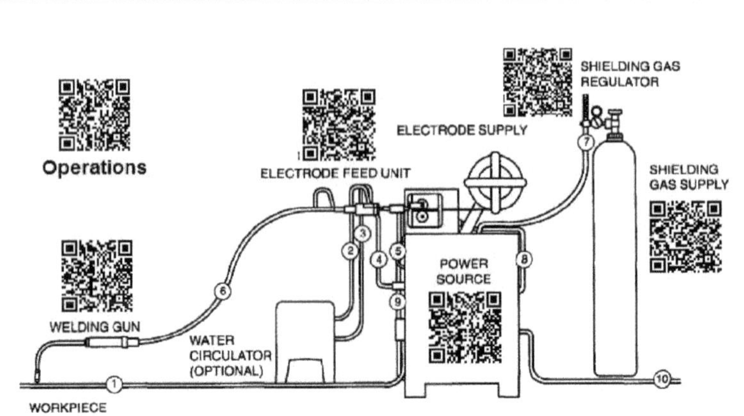

Gas Metal Arc Welding

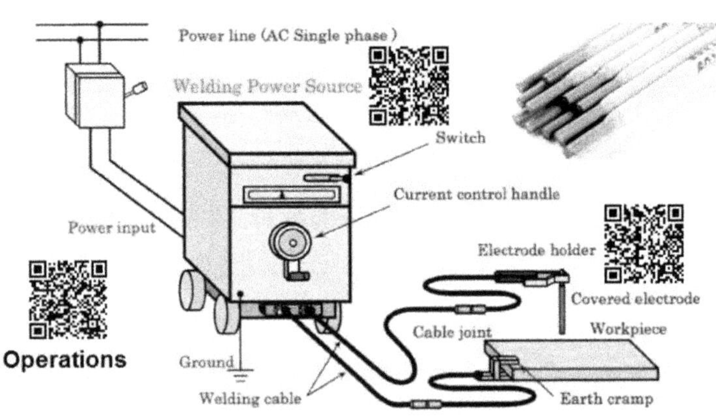

Shielded Metal Arc Welding

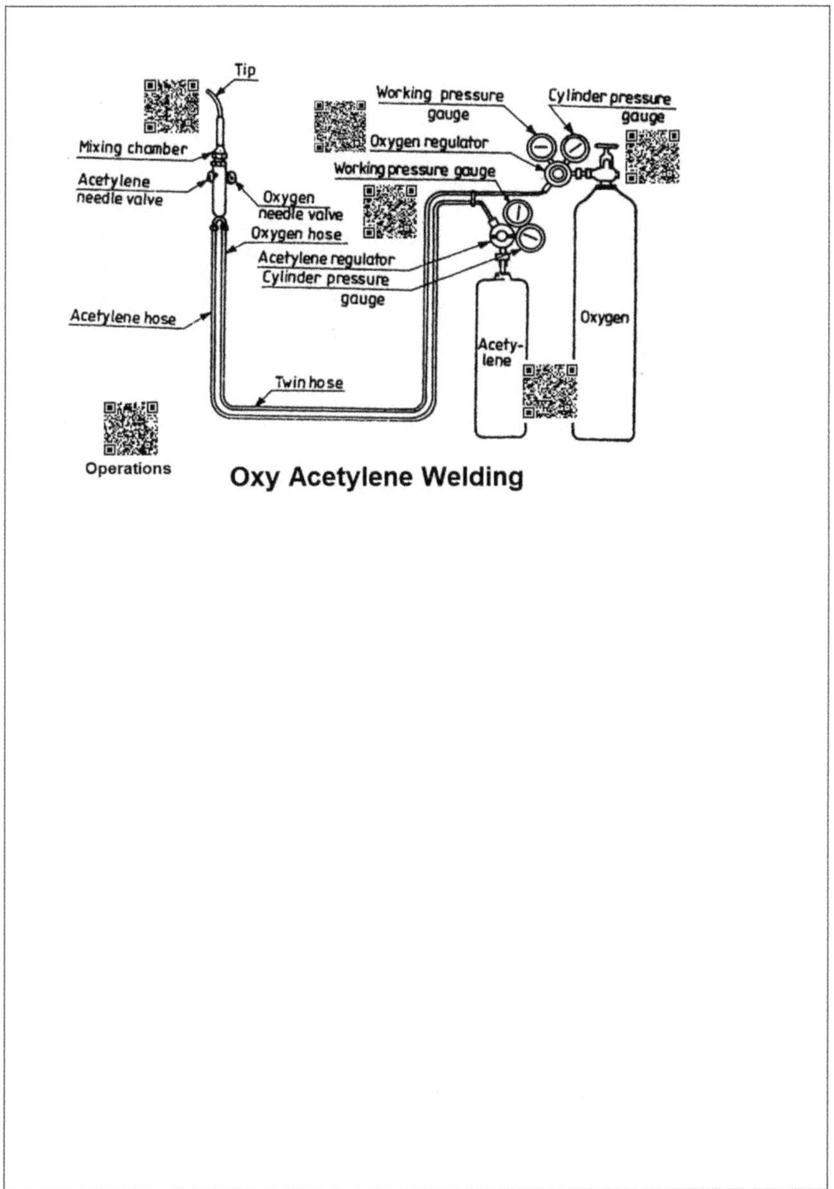

Oxy Acetylene Welding

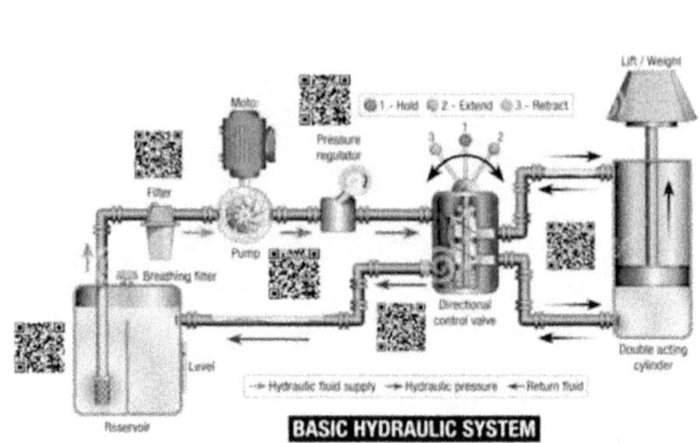

Direct Pressure Relief Valves

- The pressure relief valve provides protection against overload experienced by the actuators in a hydraulic system. One important function is to limit the force or torque produced by the hydraulic cylinders or motors.

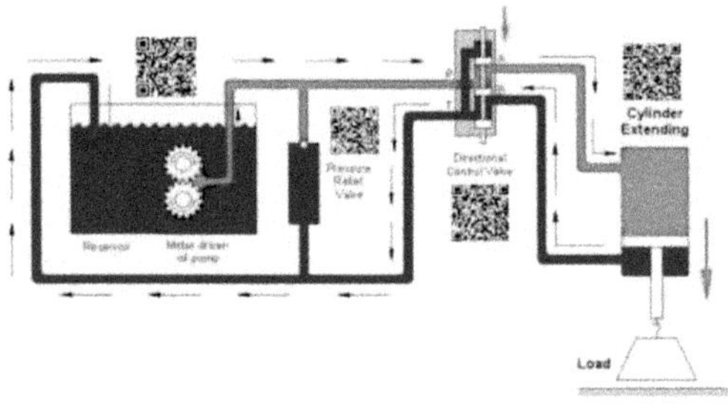

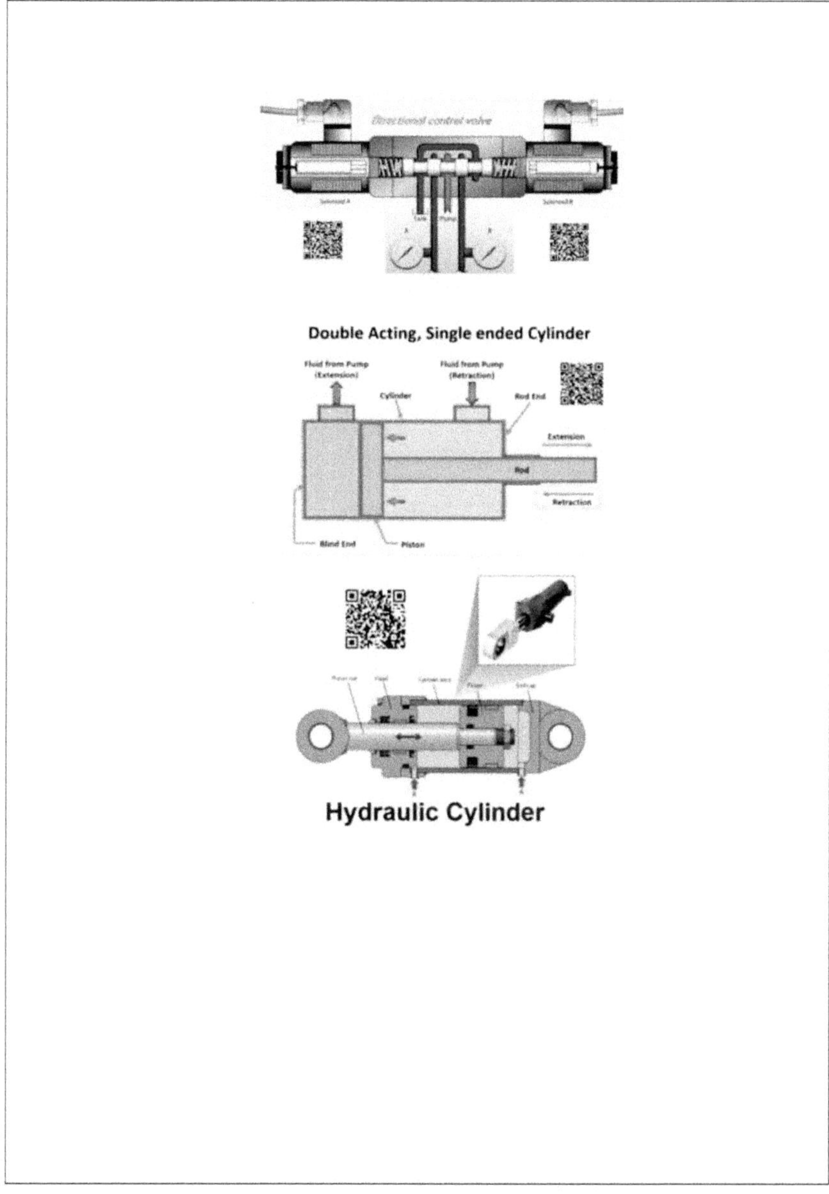
Directional control valve
Double Acting, Single ended Cylinder
Fluid from Pump
(Extension)
Fluid from Pump
(Retraction)
Cylinder
Rod End
Extension
Rod
Retraction
Blind End
Piston
Hydraulic Cylinder

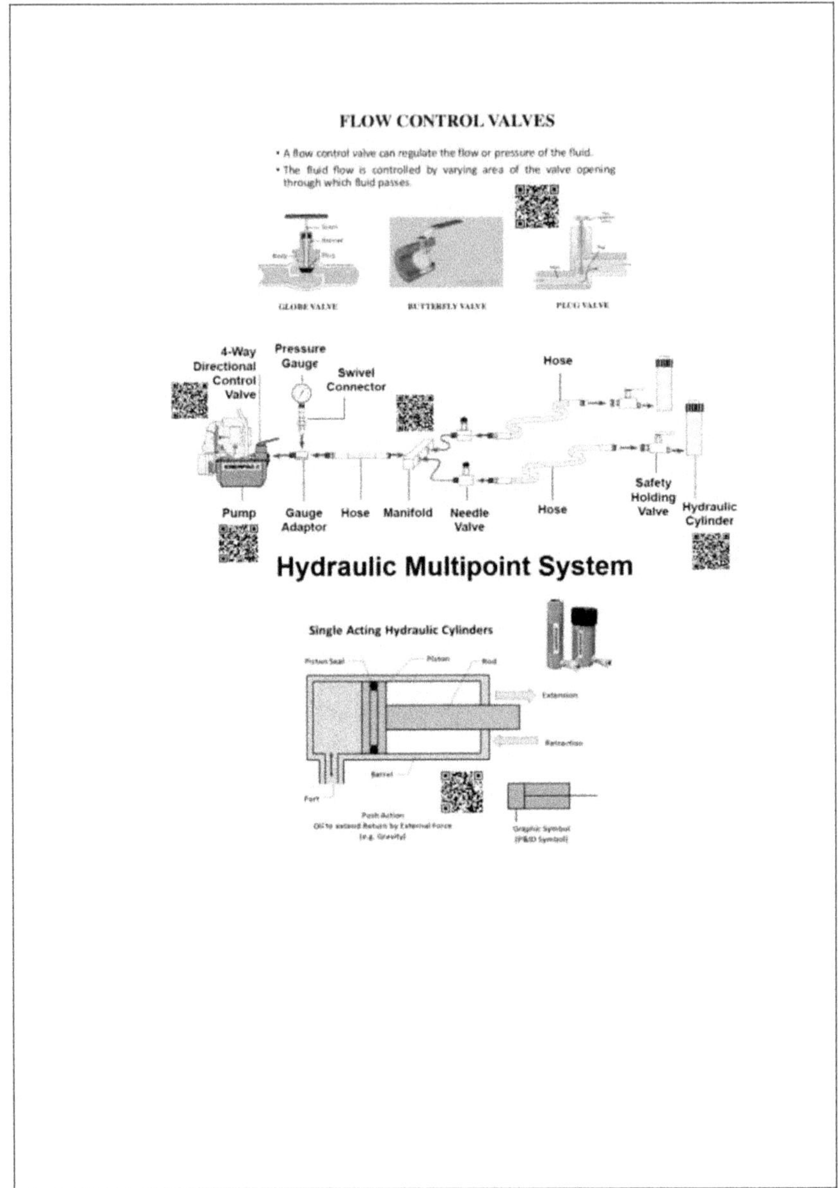
FLOW CONTROL VALVES
• A flow control valve can regulate the flow or pressure of the fluid.
• The fluid flow is controlled by varying area of the valve opening through which fluid passes.
GLOBE VALVE
BUTTERFLY VALVE
PLUG VALVE
4-Way Directional Control Valve
Pressure Gauge
Swivel Connector
Hose
Pump
Gauge Adaptor
Hose
Manifold
Needle Valve
Hose
Safety Holding Valve
Hydraulic Cylinder
Hydraulic Multipoint System
Single Acting Hydraulic Cylinders

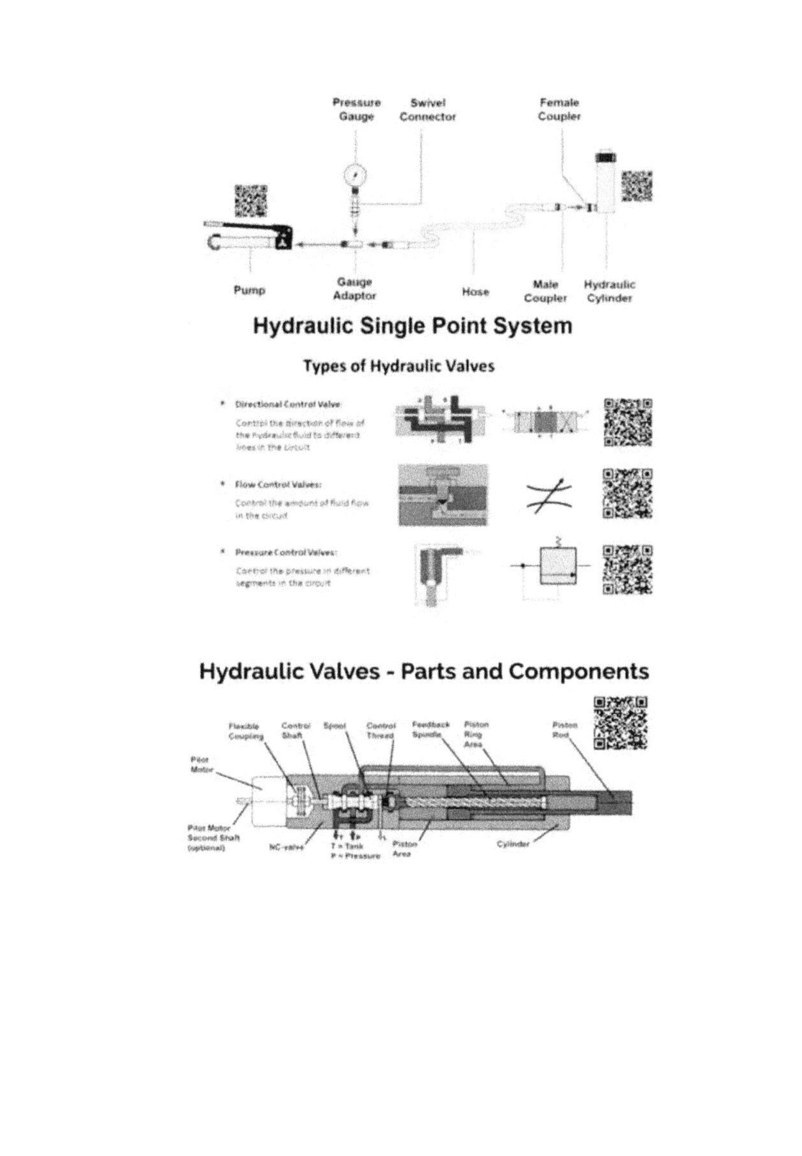
Pressure Gauge
Swivel Connector
Female Coupler
Pump
Gauge Adaptor
Hose
Male Coupler
Hydraulic Cylinder
Hydraulic Single Point System
Types of Hydraulic Valves
Directional Control Valve:
Control the direction of flow of the hydraulic fluid to different lines in the circuit
Flow Control Valves:
Control the amount of fluid flow in the circuit
Pressure Control Valves:
Control the pressure in different segments in the circuit
Hydraulic Valves - Parts and Components
Flexible Coupling
Control Shaft
Spool
Control Thread
Feedback Spindle
Piston Ring Area
Piston Rod
Pilot Motor
Pilot Motor Second Shaft (optional)
NC-valve
T = Tank
P = Pressure
Piston Area
Cylinder

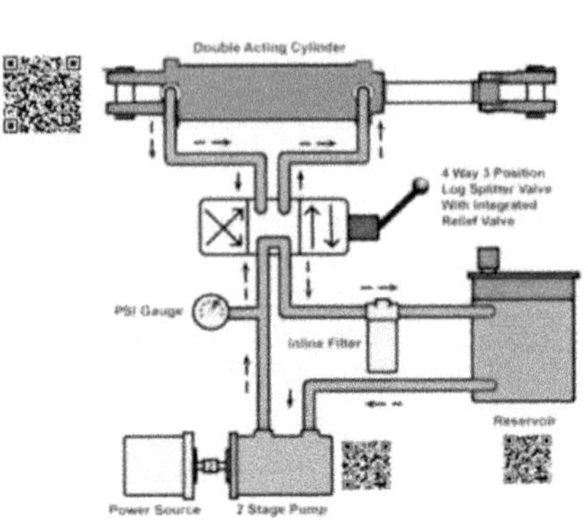

Hydraulic Double Acting Cylinder

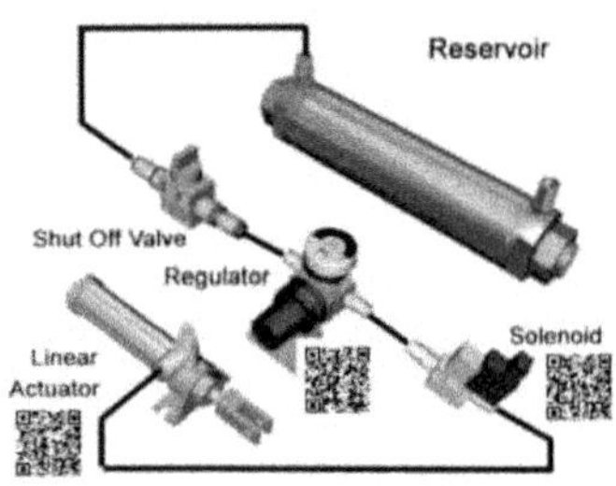

Pneumatic System

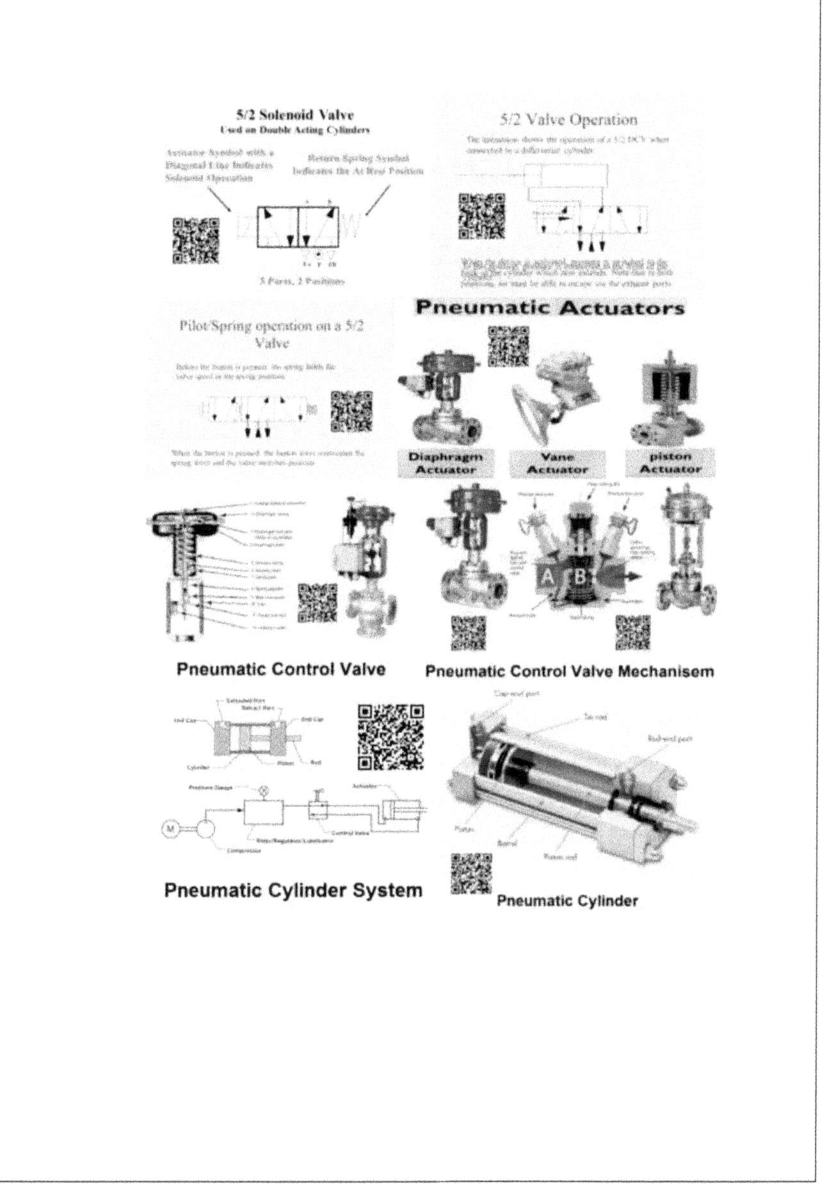
5/2 Solenoid Valve
Used on Double Acting Cylinders
5/2 Valve Operation
Pneumatic Actuators
Pilot/Spring operation on a 5/2 Valve
Diaphragm Actuator
Vane Actuator
piston Actuator
Pneumatic Control Valve
Pneumatic Control Valve Mechanisem
Pneumatic Cylinder System
Pneumatic Cylinder

CHAPTER TWO

Pump Operator cum Mechanic MCQ

1] Which one is a workshop safety?

A] Keep shop floor clean and free from grease, oil or other slippery materials

B] Stop the machine before changing the speed

C] Don't use cracked or chipped tools

D] Don't try to stop a running machine with hand

2] In Personal Protect Equipment (PPE] HELMET is used to

A] protect head

B] Protect eyes

C] Protect hands

D] Protect ears

3] Which of the following belongs to general safety?

A Have a worker in good attitude

B] The work clean and clear

C] Concentrate on your work

D] Keep the floor and gangways clean and clear

4] While grinding, which is used to protect the eyes?

A] Dark green glass

B] Mask

C] Sun glasses

D] Safety goggles

5] Which of the following is done for machine safety?

A] Check the oil level before starting the machine

B] Do things in a methodical way

C] Keep the floor and gangways clean and clear

D] Don't use dies and scarves

6] In Personal Protect Equipment (PPE], 'sleeves' is used to protect ----------

A] Face

B] Eyes

C] Ears

D] Hands

7] ABC stands for --------------

A] Automatic Breathing Control

B] Automatic Blood Control

C] Airway Breathing Circulation

D] Automatic Blood Circulation

8] Fire & FIRE EXTINGUISHERS

Fire extinguisher

9] To put off"Class B" fire, the types of fire extinguisher used is ....

A] dry power

B] Carbon dioxide

C] Jet of water

D] Foam type

10] Which type of fire extinguisher is used to put off general fire?

A] Water type Extinguisher

B] Foam type Extinguisher

C] Dry chemical powder Extinguisher

D] Carbon dioxide (C02] Extinguisher

11] In case of bleeding, take treatment Of

D] cold 3" and rest

A] spray cold water

B] Bandage immediately -----.

B] Enquire about the accident thought treatment

12] in case of an accident, the victim should im
A] Asked to take rest
C] Attended immediately
D] leave him
13] First aid is given to an injured or ill person primarily....
A] Save life
B] Prevent further deterioration of the muff's
C] Give best possible comfort
D] All of these
14] Colour code for Bins for waste paper segregation is -----
A] blue Colour
B] Yellow Colour
C] Red Colour
D] Green Colour
15] In Japanese Seiko stands for -------------
A] Shine
B] Sort
C] Standardize
D] Sustain
16] Benefit of SS system is ------
A] Increase in productivity
B] Increase in quality
C] Reduction in wastage of time
D] All of these
17] Safety is -----------
A] nobody's business
B] every bodise business
C] Some bodies business
D] The organization business
18] For basic categories of safety signs are available The meaning of"prohibition" sign ----

A] shows it must not be done
B] Shows what must be done
C] Warns the hazard or danger
D] Gives information of safety provision
18] One micrometer (U] is equal to...
A] 0.1mm
B] 0.01mm
C] 0.001mm
D] 0.0001mm
19] The caliper meant for measuring the width of a slot is...
A] Odd leg caliper
B] Outside caliper
C] Jenny caliper
D] Inside calliper

Calliper

20] The size of the dividers are specified by the ----------
A] Total length of legs
B] Distance between the points when fully opened
C] Length of legs without points
D] distance between the pivot and the point
21] The instrument used to mark parallel lines, parallel to the datum edge is -
A] jenny caliper
B] Divider
C] Outside calliper
D] Inside calliper
22] Which one of the following is an indirect measuring tool?
A] Outside caliper
B] Vernier calliper
C] Steel rule

D] Outside micrometer

23] For cutting thin tubing, the most suitable pitch of the hacksaw blade is...

A] 1.8mm

B] 1.4mm

C] 1mm

D] 0.8mm

24] For cutting solid brass, the most suitable pitch of the hacksaw blade is...

A] 1.8mm

B] 1.4mm

C] 1mm

D] 0.8mm

Hacksaw frame

25] A new hacksaw blade after a few strokes becomes loose because of the...

A] Stretching of the blade

B] Wing-nut threads being worn out

C] Wrong pitch of the blade

D] Improper selection of the set of saws.

26] While cutting small diameter pipes, it is advisable to watch regularly and ensure that...

A] The cut is along the curved line

B] More saw teeth are in contract

C] The work is not overheated

D] Proper balancing of hacksaw is maintained

27] The vice clamps are used to...

A] Protect hard jaws

B] Clamp the work pieces rigidly

C] Protect the finished surfaces

D] Prevent the movable jaw being filed

28] The reference surface during marking is provided by the...

A] Surface gauge

B] Workpiece

C] Drawing of the work

D] Marking table surface

29] The size of an engineer's vice is specified by the...

A] Length of the movable jaw

B] Width of the jaws

C] Height of the vice

D] Maximum opening of the jaws

30] The part of the universal surface gauge which helps to draw a parallel line along a datum edge is the..

A] Rocker arm

B] Snug

C] Fine adjustment screw

D] Guide pins

Universal surface guage

31] Scribers are made of...

A] Mild steel

B] High carbon steel

C] Brass

D] Cast iron

32] Portion of the hammer used for fixing the handle is...

A] Face

B] Peen
C] Cheek
D] Eye hole
33] Weight of the hammer for the marking purpose is...
A] 250g
B] 500g
C] 1 kg
D] 2 kgs

Hammer

34] The size of the dividers are specified by the...
A] Total length of the legs
B] Distance between the points when fully opened
C] Length of legs without the points
D] Distance between the pivot and the point
35] The included angle of the groove of 'V' block is always....
A] 45°
B] 60°
C] 90°
D] 120°
36] 'V' blocks are available in grades of...
A] A & B
B] A,B & C
C] 1,2 & 3
D] 1 & 2
37] 'V' blocks of grade 'B' are made of
A] Cast iron
B] Mild steel
C] Steel

D] Cast steel

38] Name the punch used to locate the centre.

A] Prick punch 30°

B] Prick punch 60°

C] Centre punch

D] Dot punch

Centre punch

39] The point angle of centre punch is --------

A] 30°

B] 50°

c] 900

D] 1200

40] Punches are used for forming ---------of any shape

A] Holes

B] Mining

C] Knurling

D] Reaming

41] Generally the length of the handle of the vice is ----------

A] 1.5 times the normal size of the vice

B] 2.5 times the normal size of the vice

C] 3.5 times the normal size of the vice

D] 4.5 times the normal size of the vice

Bench vice

42] Bench vice spindle is made of ....

A] mild steel

B] Cast iron

C] Tool steel

D] Bronze

43] The convexity of files helps...

A] To file concave surfaces

B] To file convex surfaces

C] To prevent rounding of edges of work

D] The file to become straight when pressure is applied

Files

44] Which file used for filling wood, leather and other soft material? .

A] Single cut file

B] Double cut file

c] Rasp cut file

D] Curved cut file

45] File used is used for ------------

A] Cleaning the work piece

C] Renewing the file teeth

B] cleaning the file teeth

D] Cleaning the chips

46] File card is used to --------

A] Clean the work piece

C] Renew the file teeth

B] Clean the file teeth

47] The point angle of scriber is -----------

A] 30°

B] 60°

C] 5° to 10°

D] 12° to 15°

48] The cutting angle for chipping cast iron is...

A] 37.5°

B] 55°

C] 60°

D] 90°

49] The chisel will dig into the material when...

A] The rake angle is more

B] The clearance angle is too low

C] The angle of inclination is more

D] The angle of inclination is too low

50] A slight convexity is given to the cutting edge to...

A] Cut curved surfaces

B] Cut sharp corners

C] Prevent digging of the ends

D] Allow the lubricant to enter

51] Surface plates are made of...

A] High grade cast steel

B] Fine-grained cast iron

C] Alloy steels

D] Wrought iron

52] Surface plates are specified by their length and breadth & are in
A] decimetre
B] Cubic meter
C] Cylindrical
53] Ribs are given on the unmachined portion of the angle plate for...
A] Easy handling
B] Convenience in manufacturing
C] Clamping while setting on machines
D] Rigidity and to prevent distortion
54] The slots on the angle plate are given for...
A] Reducing weight
B] Aligning the work
C] Lifting using hooks
D] Accommodating bolts.
55] The size of the angle plates is stated by...
A] Weight
B] Length
C] Length x width
D] Size number
56] for high speed parting off work on material like cemented carbide Is'
A] Do all machine
B] Cutting off machine
C] Heavy duty power saw
D] Mining machine sitting saw
57] Gun metal is an alloy of copper, ------------
A] tin and zinc
B] Lead and zinc
C] Zinc and nickel
D] Lead and nickel
58] Cast iron is used for manufacturing machine beds because -------

A] it can resist more compressive stress

B] it is heavy in weight

C] It is cheaper metal

D] It is a brittle metal

59] Accuracy or least count of a metric outside micrometric is ---------

A] 0-1 mm

B] 0.01 mm

C] 0.001 mm

D] 0.02 mm

60] 1000 microns means -----

A] 1 mm

B] 1 m

C] 1000 mm

D] 10 cm

61] in a metric micrometer, a complete revolution of thimble advances -----------

A] 0.01 mm

B] 0.25 mm

C] 0.50 mm

D] 1.00mm

Micrometer

62] Ratchet Stop in the micrometer helps to ------------

A] Control the pressure

B] lock the spindle

C] Adjust the zero error

D] Hold the work piece

63] 1000 micron means ------------

A] 1 mm

B] 1 m

C] 1000 mm

D] 10 cm

64] What is the zero reading of a 50-75 mm outside micrometer?

A] 0.000 mm

B] 0.01 mm

C] 25.00 mm

D] 50.00 mm

65] The value of the smallest division on sleeve of a metric outside micrometer is -----

A] 0.50 mm

B] 1.00 mm

C] 1.50 mm

D] 2.00 mm

66] Ratchet stop in the micrometer helps to ---------

A] control the pressure

B] Lock the spindle

C] Adjust the zero error

D] Hold the work piece

67] Least count of depth micrometer is

A] 0.5 mm

B] 0.2 mm

C] 0.001 mm

D] 0.01 mm

Depth micrometer

68] The least count of vernier calliper is (main scale = 49 division, vernier scale = 50 division]

A] 0.1 mm

B] 0.01 mm

C] 0.001 mm

D] 0.02 mm

Vernier Calliper

69] The type of measurement made by using a Vernier Calliper is -------

A] Direct measurement

B] Indirect measurement

C] 90“] (a] 81 (b]

D] None of these

70] The least count of a vernier bevel protractor is...

A] 1”

B] 5’

C] 1◦

D] 5 ◦

71] The part of a vernier bevel protractor which is normally used as a reference base for measuring angles is the...

A] Blade

B] <u>Stock</u>

C] Disc

C] Main scale

Vernier bevel protractor

72] The part of a vernier bevel protector on which main scale divisions are marked is the...

A] Stock

B] Dial

C] <u>Disc</u>

D] Adjustable blade

73] The part of a bevel protractor, which comes in contact with the inclined surface while measuring is the...

A] <u>Blade</u>

B] Stock

C] Disc

D] Dial

74] The value of each division of the main scale of a vernier bevel protractor is...

A] 5'

B] <u>1°</u>

C] 5°

D]10°

75] The value of each division of the vernier scale of a bevel protractor is...

A] 1°

B] 1◦5'

C] <u>1◦55'</u>

D] 5'

76] The taper shank drills are held on the machine by means of...

A] Chucks

<u>B] Sleeves</u>

C] Drift

D] Vice

77] Drill chucks are fitted on the drilling machine spindle by means of a...

A] Knurled ring

<u>B] Arbor</u>

C] Drift

D] Pinion and key

78] The Morse taper provided on drills ranges between...

A] <u>MT 1 to MT 5</u>

B] MT 1 to MT 4

C] MT 0 to MT 5

D] MT 0 to MT 4

79] A drift is used for...

A] Drawing a drill location

B] Fixing chuck on the machine spindle

C] Removing a broken drill from the work

D] <u>Removing the drill from the machine spindle</u>

80] When the taper shank of the drill is larger than the machine spindle, the device to hold the drill is a...

A] Drill sleeve

B] <u>Taper socket</u>

C] Drill drift

D] Chuck and key

81] The suitable cutting fluid for drilling mild steel in a drilling machine is...

A] Synthetic soluble oil
B] Neat oil
C] Distilled water
D] Soluble oil

82] A special feature of the radial drilling machine is...
A] It can be used for drilling with a H.S.S. drill
B] Table can be moved and set at any position
C] A variety of speeds is available
D] The spindle can be brought to any position

83] The point angle of drills depends on...
A] The size of the drill
B] The type of machine
C] The material of the work
D] The RPM of the drill

84] The point angle for a standard drill is...
A] 60°
B] 108°
C] 118°
D] 135°

85] The helical angle determines the...
A] Cutting angle
B] Chew angle
C] Rake angle
D] Lip angle

86] The clearance angle of the drill is between...
A] 3° to 5°
B] 8° to 12°

C] 12° to 20°

D] 15° to 20°

87] In a remote place (no electricity available] a rail track is to be drilled. Choose the right drilling machine

A] Radial drilling machine

B] Pillar drilling machine

C] Ratchet drilling machine

D] Sensitive drilling Machine

Drilling

88] A drilling machine used by a carpenter for cabinet making is a...

A] Ratchet drilling machine

B] Radial drilling machine

C] Breast drilling machine

D] Sensitive drilling machine

89] Which one of the following drilling machines is used for drilling holes where electricity is not available?

A] Bench drilling machine

B] Pillar drilling machine

C] Redial drilling machine

D] Ratchet drilling machine

90] Which one of the following drilling machine is used for heavy duty work?

A] Bench drilling machine

B] Pillar drilling machine

C] Radial drilling machine

D] Electric hand drilling machine

91] Drill chuck are held on the machine spindle by means of ------

A] arbor

B] Drift

C] draw-in bar

D] Chuck nut

92] Different speeds are obtained in a sensitive bench drilling machine by ----

A] Belt pulley mechanism

B] Hydraulic mechanism

C] Rack and Pinion mechanism

D] Cam and follower mechanism

93] The process of heating and cooling to change the structure of steel for obtaining the required properties is called

A] Hardening

B] Normalizing

C] Heat treatment

D] Tempering

94] The main purpose of annealing is to

A] Increase the hardness

B] Increase the toughness

C] Improve machinability

D] Improve distortion

95] The purpose of normalizing steel is to -----------

A] Remove the induced Stress

B] Improve genes and reduce brittleness

C] Soften the metal

D] Increase the surface?

96] Which one of the following process is used for hardenmg the outer 5" Annealing

A] Hardening

B] Tempering

C] Case Hardening

D] Tear surface

97] The purpose of producmg a component with tough and ductIle core and hard ou is known as......

A] Hardening

B] Case hardening

C] Tempering

D] annealing

98] Lower critical temperature of high carbon steel while hardening is ----------

A] 9600C

B] 900°C

c] 7230 c

D] 56O C

99] The process of Changing the structure and thus changing the properties by heating and 'cooling is known as

A] Heat treatment

B] Alloying

C] Tempering

D] None of these

100] For refining the grain structure which one of the following heat treatment processes 'Is adopted.

A] Annealing

B] Hardening

C] Tempering

D] Normalising

101] Annealing is performed on iron and steel ---------

A] To remove internal stresses

B] To reduce hardness

C] To improve machinability

D] All of these

102] Which one of the following does not fall under the stages of heat treatment?

A] Heating

B] Cleaning

C] Quenching

D] Soaking

20] METAL 02

103] Gun metal is an alloy of copper, ------------

A] tin and zinc

B] Lead and zinc

C] Zinc and nickel

D] Lead and nickel

104] for making gutters, roof flashing, hoods etc.

A] Galvanised iron

B] Stainless steel

C] Copper sheet

D] Metal sheets

105] in dairies. food processing, kitchen ware etc.
A] Galvanised iron
B] Stainless steel
C] Copper sheet
D] Metal sheets

106] for making buckets, heating ducts, cabinets etc.
A] Galvanised iron
B] Stainless steel
C] Copper sheet
D] Metal sheets

107] Punching a number of holes in a sheet is known as?
a) Perforating
b) Parting
c) Notching
d) Lancing

108] Shearing the sheet into two or more pieces is known as?
a) Perforating
b) Parting
c) Notching
d) Lancing

109] Removing the pieces from the edge in shearing operation is known as?
a) Perforating
b) Parting
c) Notching
d) Lancing

110] Leaving a tab without removing any material is known as?
a) Perforating
b) Parting
c) Notching
d) Lancing

111] Moving a small straight punch up and down rapidly into a die is done by a process known as?
a) Perforating
b) Parting
c) Nibbling
d) Lancing

112] As the thickness of sheet is increased the clearance needed will also?

a) Increase

b) Decrease

c) No effect

d) First decrease then increase

113] Bevelling is particularly suitable for shearing of?

a) Thin blanks

b) Thick blanks

c) Very thin blanks

d) None of the Mentioned

114] Which of the following is a type of die?

a) Simple dies

b) Progressive dies

c) Compound die

d) All of the Mentioned

115] Which of the following die can perform multiple operations such as blanking, punching, notching etc.?

a) Simple dies

b) Progressive dies

c) Compound die

d) None of the Mentioned

116] As the clearance increases, the punch force required?

a) Decreases

b) Increases

c) Remains same

d) First increases then decrease

117] Maximum temperature for forging H. S. S. is -------------degree.

A] 1200

B] 100

C] 1100

D] 1500

118] Main purpose Of annealing is -----------.

A] to improve machinability

B] to improve magnetism

C] to increase hardness

D] to increase toughness

119] The carbon percentage in H.S.S. tool is -------

A] 0.75 to 1.00 %

B] 1.00 to 2.00 00

C] 0.60 to 0.75 %

D] 0.02 to 0.03 %.

120] Which one of the following is the resistance of a metal to elastic deformation?

A] Ductility.

B] Strength

C] Stiffness

D] Toughness

121] in canneries and chemical plants Metal sheets

A] Galvanised iron

B] Stainless steel

C] Copper sheet

D] Metal sheets

122] Alloy steel, good corrosive resistance and welds easily

A] Black iron

B] Galvanised iron

C] Stainless steel

D] Aluminium

123] Cheapest, can be rolled to any desired thickness

A] Black iron

B] Galvanised iron

C] Stainless steel

D] Aluminium

124] Resists against rust bright silvery appearance

A] Black iron

B] Galvanised iron

C] Stainless steel

D] Aluminium

125] Corrodes rapidly. Bluish black appearance

A] Black iron

B] Galvanised iron

C] Stainless steel

D] Aluminium

126] Drill a blind hole equal to half of the diameter of the stud. Insert this tool into the hole and remove the stud by turning this anticlockwise.

A] Prick Punch Method

B] Filing square very mm

C] Using square taper punch

D] Ezy-out method

127] If the stud is broken near to the surface, employ this method to remove the stud.

A] Prick Punch Method

B] Filing square very mm

C] Using square taper punch

D] Ezy-out method

128] When a stud is broken a little above the surface this method is used to remove the stud.

A] Filing square very mm

B] Using square taper punch

C] Ezy-out method

D] Making drill hole

129] To extract the broken stud a special tool is employed in this method.

A] Prick Punch Method

B] Filing square very mm

C] Using square taper punch

D] Ezy-out method

130] File the protruding stud into square form and remove it.

A] Prick Punch Method

B] Filing square very mm

C] Using square taper punch

D] Ezy-out method

131] Ammonium chloride is used as a flux for soldering...

A] steel

B] aluminium

C] galvanized iron

D] stainless steel

132] Soldering of M.S sheets takes place at a temperature of...

A] 150◦C

B] 250◦C

C] 400◦C

D] 850◦C

133.] In soldering operation the base metal is...

A.] not heated

B.] heated to 200◦C

C.] heated to 650◦C

D.] heated to red hot condition

134] Rivets for Joining sheets to thick plates.

A] Countersunk head

B] Flat head

C] Pan head

D] Mushroom

135] Rivets for Joining sheet metal.

A] Countersunk head

B] Flat head

C] Pan head

D] Mushroom

136] Rivets for Heavy fabrication work.

A] Countersunk head

B] Flat head

C] Pan head

D] Mushroom

137] Rivets for Reduces the height of rivet head above the meta\ surface

A] Countersunk head

B] Flat head

C] Pan head

D] Mushroom

138] Rivets for commonly used for structural work.

A] Countersunk head

B] Flat head

C] Pan head

D] Snap head

139] The pressure of acetylene gas for gas cutting a 10mm M.S plate is...

A.] 0.15 kgf/cm2

B.] 0.5 kgf/cm2

C.] 1.0 kgf/cm2

D.] 1.5 kgf/cm2

140] What size of the cutting nozzle you will select for cutting 10mm thick mild steel?

A.] 0.8 mm

B.] 1.2 mm

C.] 1.6 mm

D.] 2.0 mm

141] The angle of filler rod in case of rightward welding technique is...

A.] 10 to 20◦

B.] 20 to 30◦

C.] 30 to 40◦

D.] 40 to 50◦

142] One of the advantages of the high pressure system of gas welding is...

A.] it is cheaper

B.] it is portable

C.] it is less dangerous

D.] it does not require a skilled welder

143] The function of a gas regulator is...

A.] get different types of flames

B.] mix the gases in the required proportion

C.] change the volume of gas flowing to the blow pipe

D.] set the working pressure

144] For welding a lap fillet joint in vertical position by gas what should be the angle of below pipe to the line of weld?

A.] 30◦ to 40◦

B.] 45◦to 50◦

C.] 60◦ to 70◦

D.] <u>75◦ to 80◦</u>

145] Which metal pipe should NOT be used for passing acetylene gas in order to avoid explosions?

A.] galvanized iron

B.] stainless steel

C.] mild steel

D.] <u>cooper</u>

146] he percentage of carbon in acetylene gas is...

A.] 99%

B.] <u>92.3%</u>

C.] 89.1%

D.] 85.3%

147] Acetylene gas contains

A.] calcium, carbon and hydrogen

B.] calcium and hydrogen

C.] calcium, carbon, hydrogen and oxygen

D.] carbon and hydrogen

148] In an acetylene purifier the sulphureted and phosphorated hydrogen are removed by...

A.] pumice

B.] water

C.] filter wool

D.] purifying chemicals

149] One of the functions of flux in gas welding is...

A.] dissolve the metal oxides

B.] reduce the melting point of mental

C.] increase the flame temperature

D.] increase the root penetration

150] On which of the following factors, the choice of flux for gas welding depend?

A.] type of material to be joined

B.] type of edge penetration

C.] type of fuel gas

D.] type of flame used

151] The divergence allowance required for gas welding a 300mm long copper butt joint is...

A.] 1 to 2 mm

B.] 2 to 3 mm

C.] 3 to 4 mm

D.] 4 to 5 mm

152] The type of edge preparation done for gas welding a 4mm thick copper butt joint is...

A.] single bevel

B.] single V

C.] double V

D.] square

153] The size of nozzle used to gas weld 3.15 mm thick aluminium butt joint is...

A.] 13
B.] 10
C.] 7
D.] 5

154] What is the value of preheating temperature for gas welding of aluminium?

A.] 100 to 120◦C
B.] 150 to 180◦C
C.] 180 to 200◦C
D.] 210 to 250◦C

155] Name the tool used to make and finish the leak proof joints of a pipe T joint

A.] groover
B.] setting hammer
C.] creasing hammer
D.] round bottom stake

156] The angle of vee groove of a single vee but joint for cast iron welding is...

A.] 60◦
B.] 70◦
C.] 80◦
D.] 90◦

157] Shielded metal arc welding is classified under the process of...

A.] electric resistance welding
B.] special welding
C.] electric arc welding
D.] electro gas welding

158] How to specify the size of an electrode holder?

A.] by its weight
B.] by its shape
C.] by its current carrying capacity
D.] by the metal used for making it

159] The current set for a 3.15mm medium coated mild steel electrode is...

A.] 50 to 80 amp
B.] 90 to 120 amp
C.] 120 to 150 amp

D.] 150 to 170 amp

160] A long arc is used in...

A.] welding with a low hydrogen electrode

B.] horizontal position

C.] plug or slot welding

D.] cast iron welding

161] If the travel speed of electrode is high, which type of weld defect you will get on a T fillet joint?

A.] overlap

B.] slag inclusion

C.] excessive reinforcement

D.] lack of root penetration

162] Which weld defect occurs on a lap fillet joint due to improper weaving of the electrode in the covering/final run?

A.] crack

B.] undercut

C.] lack of fusion

D.] edge of plate melted off

163] Which one of the following is used in the oxy-arc cutting process?

A.] flux coated solid electrode

B.] bare wire tubular electrode

C.] flux coated tubular electrode

D.] bare tungsten arc cutting electrode

164] The electrode holder in a carbon arc cutting equipment is made up of...

A.] plain carbon steel

B.] galvanized iron

C.] aluminium

D.] copper

165] The taper shank drills are held on the machine by means of...

A. Chucks

B. Sleeves

C. Drift

D. Vice

166] Drill chucks are fitted on the drilling machine spindle by means of a...

A.] Knurled ring

B.] Arbor

C.] Drift

D.] Pinion and key

167] The Morse taper provided on drills ranges between...

A.] MT 1 to MT 5

B.] MT 1 to MT 4

C.] MT 0 to MT 5

D.] MT 0 to MT 4

168] A drift is used for...

A.] Drawing a drill location

B.] Fixing chuck on the machine spindle

C.] Removing a broken drill from the work

D.] Removing the drill from the machine spindle

169] When the taper shank of the drill is larger than the machine spindle, the device to hold the drill is a...

A.] Drill sleeve

B.] Taper socket

C.] Drill drift

D.] Chuck and key

170] The process of enlarging the end of a hole for accommodating the socket screw head is...

A.] Reaming

B.] Spot facing

C.] Counter boring

D.] Counter sinking

171] Appropriate tool used for spot facing operation is...

A.] Reamer

B.] Counter sinks

C.] Fly cutters

D.] Lathe tool

172] Centre drilling is an operation of...

A.] Drilling and countersinking

B.] Drilling and counter boring

C.] Marking the centre location before drilling

D.] Enlarging the diameter of a hole

173] A short reamer with an axial hole used with an arbor or mandrel is called -------

A] Parallel reamer

B] Adjustable reamer

C] Expansion reamer

<u>D] Chucking reamer</u>

Reamer

174] Which one of the following machine reamers is used to correct the misalignment between the reamer axis and the work axis?

<u>A] Floating blade reamer</u>

B] Machine jig reamer.

C] Shell reamer

D] Chucking reamer

175] Tap are re sharpened by grinding -----

<u>A] Hutes</u>

B] Threads

C] Diameter

D] Relief

176] 50 metric coarse thread is designated as M12 x 125 What does '12' indicate?

<u>A] Major diameter</u>

B] Root diameter

C] Pitch diameter

D] Blank diameter

177] find the change gears required to cut a 3 mm pitch on 3 lat ' mm pitch 120

A] Driver / Driven =.455/120

<u>B] Driver/ Driven = 60/120</u>

C] Driver / Driven = 80/120

D] Driver/ Driven 2 40/80 of 5 mm

178] calculate the gears required to cut a 1 5 mm pitch on a lathe havmg lead screw Pitch

A] Driver / Driven -_20/100

<u>B] Driver/ Driven = 30/100</u>

C] Driver / Driven = 40/120

D] Driver/ Driven = 60/120

179] the top surface joining the two sides of adjacent thread is called

A] Crest

B] Root

C] Flank

D] Thread is angle

Thread

180] The included angle of the ISO metric thread is --------

A] 27 1 /2°

B] 30°

C] 55°

D] 60°

181] Which one of the following screw thread forms has an included angle of 55° between the flanks of threads?

A] B. A. Thread

B] Acme thread

C] Buttress threads

D] Knuckle thread

182] Which one of the following is used only for finishing and maintaining correct form of thread?

A] Tap

B] Threading tool

C] Threading chaser

D] Tipped tool

183] The angle 0f lS thread (V shaped] is ----------

A] 29°

B] 47 1/4°

C] 50°

D] 60

184] ln which of the following methods, only external threads are made -------

A] Form tool mEthOd

B] Compound rest method

C] Tailstock offset method

D] Taper turning attachment method.

185] The surface joining the crest and the root of a thread is known as ----

A] Flank

B] Shank

C] Pitch surface

D] All Of these

186] Pitch of a two start thread is 4 mm. Then the lead of the thread is given by -----

A] 4mm

B] 2mm

C] 8mm

D] 6mm

187] The Gear ratio required for cutting a screw thread of 2.5 mm on a lathe having a lead screw pitch using single point cutting tool is ----

A] 1:2

B] 2:1

C] 1:1 mm

188] A die in which more than one cutting operation is per formed in one stroke

A] Piercing die

B] Progressive die

C] Combination die

D] Compound die

189] A die in which cutting and non cutting operations are carried out per stroke.

A] Piercing die

B] Progressive die

C] Combination die

D] Compound die

Tap Die

190] A die in which two or more sequential operations are performed at two or more stations upon the work.

A] Piercing die

B] Progressive die

C] Combination die

D] Compound die

191] A die in which the shape of the punch and die are directly reproduced in the metal with little or no metal flow.

A] Progressive die

B] Combination die

C] Compound die

D] Forming die

192] The die used for producing any shape of holes.

A] Piercing die

B] Progressive die

C] Combination die

D] Compound die

193] Abrasives are classifications into............

A] Two types

B] Three types

c] One types

D] Four types

194] Grinding wheels made out of---------------- abrasive are most common because of its free and cool cutting action.

A] Aluminium oxide

B] Silicon oxide

C] Ammonium oxide

D] Carbide.

195] Which among the following abrasive is mostly used for cutting off wheels for cutting non metallic materials?

A] Aluminium oxide

B] Silicon carbide

C] Diamond

D] None of above

196] Which abrasive particle is used for grinding tungsten carbide tool insert?

A] Silicon carbide

B] A|203

C] Diamond

D] Corundum

197] Which of the following is the natural abrasive?

A] Aluminium oxide

B] Silicon

C] Boron carbide

D] Corundum

198] Which of the following is the manufactured abrasive?

A] Corundum.

B] Quartz

C] Silicon

D] Emery

199] Which abrasive particle is used for grinding steel fittings?

A] Silicon carbide

B] Aluminium oxide

C] Diamond.

D] boron oxide

200] What kind of abrasive cut of wheel should be used to cut concrete stone and masonry?

A] Silicon

B] Al203

C] Diamond grit

D] Glass

201] Aluminium oxide wheel is used for grinding ------------

A] cast iron

B] Cemented carbide.

C] HSS '

D] ceramic

202] The bond of diamond wheel suitable for offhand grinding of the tipped tool is ....

A] Resinoid

B] Vitrified

C] Shellac

D] Metal

Grinding Wheel

203] Which among the following bonds, is used commonly?

A] Vitrified bond '

B] Rubber bond

C] Shellac bond

D] Silicate bond

204] The symbol conventionally used for resinoid .bond is ~~~~~~~~

A] v

B] R f

C] B

D] E

205] In grinding practice the term "grade of wheel" refers to ---------'

A] Hardness of the abrasive used

B] Strength of the bond of the wheel

C] Finish 0f the Wheel

D] Hardness of the work pieces

206] Which bond is used in cut of wheels?

A] Rubber

B] Vitrified

C] Resirjoid

D] Shellac

207] Hardness of grinding wheel is determine by ----------

A] the resistance exerted. by the bond against grinding Stress

B] Hardness of abrasive grains

C] Hardness of bond

D] Ability to penetration

208] When it is required to run a Grinding wheel safely at very high speed, which bond should be used? "

A] Vitrified

B] Shellac

C] Silicate

D] resinoid‘ and rubber

209] in surface grinding what is the suitable range of grain size of the grinding wheel for general purpose surface grinding?

A] 20 to 36

B] 46 to 60

C] 80 to 120

D] 150 to 300

210] AS per Indian Standard, the grain ’46’.comes under the group of «w. -----

A] Coarse

B] Medium

C] Fine

D] Very fine

211] The grit size of the abrasives used in the grinding wheel is usually specified by ----------

A] Hardness number

B] A size of wheel

C] Softness or hardness of the abrasive

D] Mesh number

212] Bench grinder are used for ....

A] Heavy duty work

B] Heavy and light duty work

C] Light duty work

D] Lather work

213] Bench Grinders are fitted on a ....

A] Base

B] Table.

C] Wheel guards

D] Conveyor

225] Which one of the following is important factor required to achieve the interchange ability in mass production? .

A] Geometrical accuracy.

B] Standardization

C] Dimensional accuracy

D] Surface finish

226] Interchange ability is normally applied for? _

A] Repairing of parts

B] Mass production

C] Single piece production

D] All of these

227] When tolerance given in one side of the basic dimension, it is called --------

A].Tolerance system

B] Unilateral tolerance

C] Bilateral tolerance

D] Allowance System

228] The measured Size Of the dimensions of a component as called---------

A] Basic size

B] Nominal Size

C] Allowed size

D] Actual size

229] In the drawing the dimensions of a shaft is shown 40i 0068/0042, which is the size of Shaft within the tolerance?

A] 4.0.64 mm

B] 40.042 mm

C] 40.000 mm

D] 39.998 mm

230] In Hole basic system ----------

A] The size of the shaft is made constant

B] The Size of the hole is made constant

C] Only 'allowance is given on the hole

D] The permissible tolerance are given on the hole and the Shaft

231] The Size of a component is given as 24 -0.1. What does -O.1 indicates? _

A] Upper deviation is + 0.1 mm .

B] Lower deviation is 0.0 mm

C] Fundamental deviation is 0.0 mm

D] Lower deviation is _0.1 mm

232] The tolerance of a hole iS the difference between the -------

A] Maximum hole Size and maximum Shaft size

B] Maximum hole size and maximum hole Size

C] Minimum'hole size and maximum Shaft Size

D] Minimum hole Size and minimum shaft Size

233] A hole whose lower deviation is zero is called basic hole. Which one of the following letter indicates basic hole?

A] E

B] F

C] G '

D] H

234] Which one having upper deviation zero?

A] Bassc Shaft

B] Basic hole

C] Tolerance

D] Clearance

235] A ball bearing on a shaft is type of fit? ,

A] Clearance fit

B] Driving fit

C] Shrinkage fit

D] None of the above

236] In the BIS system of limits and fits, the grade of tolerance are represented by number Symbols and there are ---------i

A] 14 grades of tolerance

B] 16 grades of tolerance

C] 18 grades of tolerance '

D] 20 grades of tolerance

237] A Product is said to have the quality when ....

Limit fit tolerance

A] Its shape and dimensions are within the

B] It is fit for use

C] It appears to be very good

D] The choice of material is right

238] The maximum clearance required between hole'30 +0.021, 0.000 and shaft 30 -0.110, 0.143 is.

A] 0.110 mm '

B]0.131 mm

C] 0.164 mm

D] 0.143 mm

239] A dimension is stated as 25 .1002 mm in a drawing. What is the tolerance?

A] +0.02 mm'

B] +0.04 mm

C] -0.02 mm

D] 25.00 mm

240] A pin is fitted in a hole. The tolerance zone of the pin is entirely above that of hole. The fit obtained will be?

A] Clearance fit

B] Transition fit

C] Interference fit

D] Running fit

241] Tolerance is given to the part size to............

A] Production the part within the required permissible size error

B] Increase the production

C] Decrease the Production

D] Finish the components approximately

242] Which one of the following is the clearance fit under the whole basic system?

A] 20 H7/p6'

B] 2067/211

C] ZOG/gll .

D] 20H/g11.

243] The three classes of fits as per BIS system aré ....

A] Clearance fit, interference fit and transition fit

B] Medium fit, push fit and tight fit

C] Flat fit, round fit and square fit

D] 'Sliding fit ', loose fit and shrinkage fit

244] Which one of the following tolerance specifications has a maximum dimensionless than 20 mm?

A] 20 +0.2,-0.3

B] 20 320.2

C] 20 -0.2, 0.3 e

D]m 20 +500, ~03

245] Difference between the maximum and minimum limit is --------------------

A] Single informant

B] Basic shaft

C] Clearance

D] Tolerance

246] A shaft 55 running freely in bush bearing the type of fit is ---------

A] Clearance fit

B] Driving plate

C] shrinkage fit

D] None of the above

256] -------------is the COFFEC'E dimension when the micrometer measures 45.54mm, if it is having a negative error of 0.02mm

A] 45.58 mm

B] 45 54 mm

C] 45.56 mm

D] 45.53 mm.

257] When the faces of the anvil and the spindle touch each other if the Zero of the Sleeve scale coincides with the zero of the thimble scale, then it is said to be -----------

A] Positive error

B] Negative error

C] Zero error

D] No error

258] Depth bar is used for measurement of --------------

A] Height.

B] Length

C] Depth

D] Inches

259] The dial test indicator shows the measurement as...

A.] The actual size of the component

B.] The difference between the two steps of 5 mm

C.] The magnified small variations in sizes through a pointer

D.] The direct reading of the dimension

260] V -block and dial indicator method is used to measure the

A] Length of the work piece ground

B] Circularity of the surface of the work piece

C] Flatness of the surface

D] Pitch of the thread

261] Which one of the following is not correct about dial test indicator?

A] It has 100 divisions on its dial

B] Motion of the stem is transferred to the dial through Gear train.

C] Its accuracy is 0.1 mm

D] Used in conjunction with depth gauge

317] Threading tools are checked for accuracy for the 60◦ angle by using a

A] Thread plug gauge

B] centre gauge

C] screw pitch gauge

D] tool angle gauge

318] The number of threads per inch can be checked with a

A] tool gauge

B] metric rule by counting

C] ring gauge

D] screw pitch gauge

screw pitch gauge

Sheet Metal MCQ

366] Which method of development is used for developing a rectangular tray?

A] triangular method

B] radial line method

C] parallel line method

D] trial and error method

367] What is the profile of the knife cutting edge of the upper blade of the hand level shear?

A] curved

B] straight

C] inclined

D] beveled

368] For what purpose a groover is used in sheet metal work?

A] to make a hem

B] to make grooves

C] to close and lock the seams

D] to strength then the edge of a job

369] Which type of stake is to be selected for making sharp bends, folding of edges of sheet metal?

A] hatchet stake

B] beak iron stake

C] square edge stake

D] tinman's anvil stake

370] Ammonium chloride is used as a flux for soldering...

A] steel

B] aluminium

C] galvanized iron

D] stainless steel

371] Name the tool used to make and finish the leak proof joints of a pipe T joint

A] groover

B] setting hammer

C] creasing hammer

D] round bottom stake

372] Which one of the following metals will not permit X-rays to pass through?

A] stainless steel

B] aluminium

C] lead

D] tin

373] The frequency of up and down vibration of the cutting edge in a nibbling machine is...

A] 1000 to 1500 times

B] 1500 to 2500 times

C] 2800 to 3000 times

D] 3000 to 3500 times

374] Name the instrument used to check the perpendicularity of the branch pipe with the main pipe of a pipe T joint

A] protractor

B] try square

C] spirit level

D] straight edge

375].Which type of notch is used when a single hem meets at right angles?

A] V notch

B] slit notch

C] slant notch

D] square notch

376] To cut out small apertures which punch and die type of machine is used?

A] shear type nibbler

B] punch type nibbler

C] circular cutting machine

D] guillotine shearing machine

377] The overheating of the blow pipe nozzle is to be avoided because it will

A] cause back fire

B] consume more oxygen and acetylene

C] create burn through defect in the joint

D] create undercut defect in the joint

378] State the nozzle size you will select to weld a 3.15mm thick mild steel sheet

A] 3

B.5

C] 7

D] 10

379] The type of flame to be set for welding brass is...

A] air acetylene flame

B] neutral flame

C] oxidizing flame

D] carburizing flame

380] What is the maximum thickness of mild steel sheet recommended for gas welding using leftward technique?

A] 12mm

B] 10mm

C] 8mm

D] 5mm

381].The distance between the root and toe of a fillet weld is called...

A] root gap

B] leg length

C] reinforcement

D] throat thickness

382] Name the weld defect which occurs due to improper cleaning of the mild steel sheet edge and surface

A] lack of root penetration

B] burn through

C] undercut

D] porosity

383] Which of the following mechanical properties of metals gives resistance to pulling forces?

A] toughness

B] ductility

C] hardness

D] tensile strength

1. The S.I. unit of power is
(a) Henry
(b) coulomb
(c) watt
(d) watt-hour
2. Electric pressure is also called
(a) resistance
(b) power
(c) voltage
(d) energy
3. The substances which have a large number of free electrons and offer a low
resistance are called
(a) insulators
(b) inductors
(c) semi-conductors
(d) conductors
4. Out of the following which is not a poor conductor ?
(a) Cast iron
(b) Copper
(c) Carbon
(d) Tungsten
5. Out of the following which is an insulating material ?
(a) Copper
(b) Gold
(c) Silver
(d) Paper
6. The property of a conductor due to which it passes current is called
(a) resistance
(b) reluctance
(c) conductance
(d) inductance
7. Conductance is reciprocal of
(a) resistance
(b) inductance
(c) reluctance
(d) capacitance
8. The resistance of a conductor varies inversely as

(a) length
(b) area of cross-section
(c) temperature
(d) resistivity
9. With rise in temperature the resistance of pure metals
(a) increases
(b) decreases
(c) first increases and then decreases
(d) remains constant
10. With rise in temperature the resistance of semi-conductors
(a) decreases
(b) increases
(c) first increases and then decreases
(d) remains constant
11. The resistance of a copper wire 200 m long is 21 Q. If its thickness (diameter)
is 0.44 mm, its specific resistance is around
(a) 1.2 x 10~8 Q-m
(b) 1.4 x 10~8 Q-m
(c) 1.6 x 10""8 Q-m
(d) 1.8 x 10"8 Q-m
13. An instrument which detects electric current is known as
(a) voltmeter
(b) rheostat
(c) wattmeter
(d) galvanometer
14. In a circuit a 33 Q resistor carries a current of 2 A. The voltage across the resistor is
(a) 33 V
(b) 66 v
(c) 80 V
(d) 132 V
15. A light bulb draws 300 mA when the voltage across it is 240 V. The resistance of the light bulb is
(a) 400 Q
(b) 600 Q
(c) 800 Q
(d) 1000 Q

16. The resistance of a parallel circuit consisting of two branches is 12 ohms. If the resistance of one branch is 18 ohms, what is the resistance of the other ?

(a) 18 Q
(b) 36 Q
(c) 48 Q
(d) 64 Q

17. Four wires of same material, the same cross-sectional area and the same length when connected in parallel give a resistance of 0.25 Q. If the same four wires are connected is series the effective resistance will be

(a) 1 Q
(b) 2 Q
(c) 3 Q
(d) 4 Q

18. A current of 16 amperes divides between two branches in parallel of resistances 8 ohms and 12 ohms respectively. The current in each branch is

(a) 6.4 A, 6.9 A
(b) 6.4 A, 9.6 A
(c) 4.6 A, 6.9 A
(d) 4.6 A, 9.6 A

19. Current velocity through a copper conductor is

(a) the same as propagation velocity of electric energy
(b) independent of current strength
(c) of the order of a few ^.s/m
(d) nearly 3 x 108 m/s

20. Which of the following material has nearly zero temperature co-efficient of resistance?

(a) Manganin
(b) Porcelain
(c) Carbon
(d) Copper

21. You have to replace 1500 Q resistor in radio. You have no 1500 Q resistor but have several 1000 Q ones which you would connect

(a) two in parallel
(b) two in parallel and one in series
(c) three in parallel
(d) three in series

22. Two resistors are said to be connected in series when

(a) same current passes in turn through both
(b) both carry the same value of current
(c) total current equals the sum of branch currents
(d) sum of IR drops equals the applied e.m.f.

23. Which of the following statement is true both for a series and a parallel D.C. circuit?
(a) Elements have individual currents
(b) Currents are additive
(c) Voltages are additive
(d) Power are additive

24. Which of the following materials has a negative temperature co-efficient of resistance?
(a) Copper
(b) Aluminum
(c) Carbon
(d) Brass

25. Ohm's law is not applicable to
(a) vacuum tubes
(b) carbon resistors
(c) high voltage circuits
(d) circuits with low current densities

26. Which is the best conductor of electricity ?
(a) Iron
(b) Silver
(c) Copper
(d) Carbon

27. For which of the following 'ampere second' could be the unit ?
(a) Reluctance
(b) Charge
(c) Power
(d) Energy

28. All of the following are equivalent to watt except
(a) (amperes) ohm
(b) joules/sec.
(c) amperes x volts
(d) amperes/volt

29. A resistance having rating 10 ohms, 10 W is likely to be a
(a) metallic resistor

(b) carbon resistor
(c) wire wound resistor
(d) variable resistor

30. Which one of the following does not have negative temperature co-efficient ?
(a) Aluminium
(b) Paper
(c) Rubber
(d) Mica

31. Varistors are
(a) insulators
(6) non-linear resistors
(c) carbon resistors
(d) resistors with zero temperature coefficient

32. Insulating materials have the function of
(a) preventing a short circuit between conducting wires
(b) preventing an open circuit between the voltage source and the load
(c) conducting very large currents
(d) storing very high currents

33. The rating of a fuse wire is always expressed in
(a) ampere-hours
(b) ampere-volts
(c) kWh
(d) amperes

34. The minimum charge on an ion is
(a) equal to the atomic number of the atom
(b) equal to the charge of an electron
(c) equal to the charge of the number of electrons in an atom (#) zero

35. In a series circuit with unequal resistances
(a) the highest resistance has the most of the current through it
(b) the lowest resistance has the highest voltage drop
(c) the lowest resistance has the highest current
(d) the highest resistance has the highest voltage drop

36. The filament of an electric bulb is made of
(a) carbon
(b) aluminium
(c) tungsten
(d) nickel

37. A 3 Q resistor having 2 A current will dissipate the power of

(a) 2 watts

(b) 4 watts

(c) 6 watts

(d) 8 watts

38. Which of the following statement is true?

(a) A galvanometer with low resistance in parallel is a voltmeter

(b) A galvanometer with high resistance in parallel is a voltmeter

(c) A galvanometer resistance in series is an ammeter with low

(d) A galvanometer with high resistance in series is an ammeter

39. The resistance of a few meters of wire conductor in closed electrical circuit is

(a) practically zero

(b) low

(c) high

(d) very high

40. If a parallel circuit is opened in the main line, the current

(a) increases in the branch of the lowest resistance

(b) increases in each branch

(c) is zero in all branches

(d) is zero in the highest resistive branch

41. If a wire conductor of 0.2 ohm resistance is doubled in length, its resistance becomes

(a) 0.4 ohm

(b) 0.6 ohm

(c) 0.8 ohm

(d) 1.0 ohm

42. Three 60 W bulbs are in parallel across the 60 V power line. If one bulb burns open

(a) there will be heavy current in the main line

(b) rest of the two bulbs will not light

(c) all three bulbs will light

(d) the other two bulbs will light

43. The four bulbs of 40 W each are connected in series swift a battery across them, which of the following statement is true ?

(a) The current through each bulb in same

(b) The voltage across each bulb is not same

(c) The power dissipation in each bulb is not same

(d) None of the above

44. Two resistances Rl and Ri are connected in series across the voltage source where Rl>Ri. The largest drop will be across

(a) Rl

(b) Ri

(c) either Rl or Ri

(d) none of them

46. A closed switch has a resistance of

(a) zero

(b) about 50 ohms

(c) about 500 ohms

(d) infinity

47. The hot resistance of the bulb's filament is higher than its cold resistance because the temperature co-efficient of the filament is

(a) zero

(b) negative

(c) positive

(d) about 2 ohms per degree

49. The insulation on a current carrying conductor is provided

(a) to prevent leakage of current

(b) to prevent shock

(c) both of above factors

(d) none of above factors

50. The thickness of insulation provided on the conductor depends on

(a) the magnitude of voltage on the conductor

(b) the magnitude of current flowing through it

(c) both (a) and (b)

(d) none of the above

51. Which of the following quantities remain the same in all parts of a series circuit ?

(a) Voltage

(b) Current

(c) Power

(d) Resistance

52. A 40 W bulb is connected in series with a room heater. If now 40 W bulb is replaced by 100 W bulb, the heater output will

(a) decrease

(b) increase

(c) remain same

(d) heater will burn out

53. In an electric kettle water boils in 10 m minutes. It is required to boil the boiler in 15 minutes, using same supply mains

(a) length of heating element should be decreased

(b) length of heating element should be increased

(c) length of heating element has no effect on heating if water

(d) none of the above

54. An electric filament bulb can be worked from

(a) D.C. supply only

(b) A.C. supply only

(c) Battery supply only

(d) All above

55. Resistance of a tungsten lamp as applied voltage increases

(a) decreases

(b) increases

(c) remains same

(d) none of the above

56. Electric current passing through the circuit produces

(a) magnetic effect

(b) luminous effect

(c) thermal effect

(d) chemical effect

(e) all above effects

57. Resistance of a material always decreases if

(a) temperature of material is decreased

(6) temperature of material is increased

(c) number of free electrons available become more

(d) none of the above is correct

58. If the efficiency of a machine is to be high, what should be low ?

(a) Input power

(b) Losses

(c) True component of power

(d) kWh consumed

(e) Ratio of output to input

59. When electric current passes through a metallic conductor, its temperature rises. This is due to

(a) collisions between conduction electrons and atoms

(b) the release of conduction electrons from parent atoms

(c) mutual collisions between metal atoms

(d) mutual collisions between conducting electrons

60. Two bulbs of 500 W and 200 W rated at 250 V will have resistance ratio as

(a) 4 : 25

(b) 25 : 4

(c) 2 : 5

(d) 5 : 2

61. A glass rod when rubbed with silk cloth is charged because

(a) it takes in proton

(b) its atoms are removed

(c) it gives away electrons

(d) it gives away positive charge

62. Whether circuit may be AC. or D.C. one, following is most effective in

reducing the magnitude of the current.

(a) Reactor

(b) Capacitor

(c) Inductor

(d) Resistor

63. It becomes more difficult to remove

(a) any electron from the orbit

(6) first electron from the orbit

(c) second electron from the orbit

(d) third electron from the orbit

64. When one leg of parallel circuit is opened out the total current will

(a) reduce

(b) increase

(c) decrease

(d) become zero

65. In a lamp load when more than one lamp are switched on the total resistance

of the load

(a) increases

(b) decreases

(c) remains same

(d) none of the above

66. Two lamps 100 W and 40 W are connected in series across 230 V (alternating).

Which of the following statement is correct ?

(a) 100 W lamp will glow brighter

(b) 40 W lamp will glow brighter

(c) Both lamps will glow equally bright

(d) 40 W lamp will fuse

67. Resistance of 220 V, 100 W lamp will be

(a) 4.84 Q

(b) 48.4 Q

(c) 484 ft

(d) 4840 Q

68. In the case of direct current

(a) magnitude and direction of current remains constant

(b) magnitude and direction of current changes with time

(c) magnitude of current changes with time

(d) magnitude of current remains constant

69. When electric current passes through a bucket full of water, lot of bubbling is observed. This suggests that the type of supply is

(a) A.C.

(b) D.C.

(c) any of above two

(d) none of the above

70. Resistance of carbon filament lamp as the applied voltage increases.

(a) increases

(b) decreases

(c) remains same

(d) none of the above

71. Bulbs in street lighting are all connected in

(a) parallel

(b) series

(c) series-parallel

(d) end-to-end

72. For testing appliances, the wattage of test lamp should be

(a) very low

(b) low

(c) high

(d) any value

73. Switching of a lamp in house produces noise in the radio. This is because switching operation produces

(a) arcs across separating contacts

(b) mechanical noise of high intensity

(c) both mechanical noise and arc between contacts

(d) none of the above

74. Sparking occurs when a load is switched off because the circuit has high

(a) resistance

(b) inductance

(c) capacitance

(d) impedance

75. Copper wire of certain length and resistance is drawn out to three times its

length without change in volume, the new resistance of wire becomes

(a) 1/9 times

(b) 3 times

(c) 9 times

(d) unchanged

76. When resistance element of a heater fuses and then we reconnect it after removing a portion of it, the power of the heater will

(a) decrease

(b) increase

(c) remain constant

(d) none of the above

77. A field of force can exist only between

(a) two molecules

(b) two ions

(c) two atoms

(d) two metal particles

78. A substance whose molecules consist of dissimilar atoms is called

(a) semi-conductor

(b) super-conducto

(c) compound

(d) insulator

79. International ohm is defined in terms of the resistance of

(a) a column of mercury

(b) a cube of carbon

(c) a cube of copper

(d) the unit length of wire

80. Three identical resistors are first connected in parallel and then in series.

The resultant resistance of the first combination to the second will be

(a) 9 times

(b) 1/9 times

(c) 1/3 times

(d) 3 times

91. Which method can be used for absolute measurement of resistances ?

(a) Lorentz method

(b) Releigh method

(c) Ohm's law method

(d) Wheatstone bridge method

92. Three 6 ohm resistors are connected to form a triangle. What is the resistance between any two corners ?

(a) 3/2 Q

(b 6 Q

(c) 4 Q

(d) 8/3 Q

93. Ohm's law is not applicable to

(a) semi-conductors

(b) D.C. circuits

(c) small resistors

(d) high currents

94. Two copper conductors have equal length. The cross-sectional area of one conductor is four times that of the other. If the conductor having smaller crosssectional area has a resistance of 40 ohms the resistance of other conductor will be

(a) 160 ohms

(b) 80 ohms

(c) 20 ohms

(d) 10 ohms

95. A nichrome wire used as a heater coil has the resistance of 2 £2/m. For a heater of 1 kW at 200 V, the length of wire required will be

(a) 80 m

(b) 60 m

(c) 40 m

(d) 20 m

96. Temperature co-efficient of resistance is expressed in terms of

(a) ohms/°C

(b) mhos/ohm°C

(c) ohms/ohm°C

98. When current flows through heater coil it glows but supply wiring does not glow because

(a) current through supply line flows at slower speed

(b) supply wiring is covered with insulation layer

(c) resistance of heater coil is more than the supply wires

(d) supply wires are made of superior material

99. The condition for the validity under Ohm's law is that

(a) resistance must be uniform

(b) current should be proportional to the size of the resistance

(c) resistance must be wire wound type

(d) temperature at positive end should be more than the temperature at negative end

100. Which of the following statement is correct ?

(a) A semi-conductor is a material whose conductivity is same as between that of a conductor and an insulator

(b) A semi-conductor is a material which has conductivity having average value of conductivity of metal and insulator

(c) A semi-conductor is one which con¬ducts only half of the applied voltage

(d) A semi-conductor is a material made of alternate layers of conducting material and insulator

101. A rheostat differs from potentiometer in the respect that it

(a) has lower wattage rating

(b) has higher wattage rating

(c) has large number of turns

(d) offers large number of tapping

102. The weight of an aluminium conductor as compared to a copper conductor of identical cross-section, for the same electrical resistance, is

(a) 50%

(b) 60%

(c) 100%

(d) 150%

103. An open resistor, when checked with an ohm-meter reads

(a) zero

(b) infinite

(c) high but within tolerance

(d) low but not zero

104. are the materials having electrical conductivity much less than most of the metals but much greater than that of typical insulators.

(a) Varistors

(b) Thermistor

(c) Semi-conductors

(d) Variable resistors

105. All good conductors have high

(a) conductance

(b) resistance

(c) reluctance

(d) thermal conductivity

106. Voltage dependent resistors are usually made from

(a) charcoal

(b) silicon carbide

(c) nichrome

(d) graphite

107. Voltage dependent resistors are used

(a) for inductive circuits

(b) to supress surges

(c) as heating elements

(d) as current stabilizers

108. The ratio of mass of proton to that of electron is nearly

(a) 1840

(b) 1840

(c) 30

(d) 4

109. The number of electrons in the outer most orbit of carbon atom is

(a) 3

(b) 4

(c) 6

(d) 7

110. With three resistances connected in parallel, if each dissipates 20 W the total power supplied by the voltage source equals

(a) 10 W

(b) 20 W

(c) 40 W

(d) 60 W

111. A thermistor has

(a) positive temperature coefficient

(b) negative temperature coefficient

(c) zero temperature coefficient

(d) variable temperature coefficient

112. If/, R and t are the current, resistance and time respectively, then according

to Joule's law heat produced will be proportional to

(a) I2Rt

(b) I2Rf

(c) I2R2t

(d) I2R2t*

113. Nichrome wire is an alloy of

(a) lead and zinc

(b) chromium and vanadium

(c) nickel and chromium

(d) copper and silver

114. When a voltage of one volt is applied, a circuit allows one micro ampere current to flow through it. The conductance of the circuit is

(a) 1 n-mho

(b) 106 mho

(c) 1 milli-mho

(d) none of the above

115. Which of the following can have negative temperature coefficient ?

(a) Compounds of silver

(6) Liquid metals

(c) Metallic alloys

(d) Electrolytes

116. Conductance : mho ::

(a) resistance : ohm

(b) capacitance : henry

(c) inductance : farad

(d) lumen : steradian

117. 1 angstrom is equal to

(a) 10-8 mm

(b) 10"6 cm

(c) <u>10"10 m</u>

(d) 10~14 m

118. One newton meter is same as

(a) one watt

(b) <u>one joule</u>

(c) five joules

(d) one joule second

1. "The mass of an ion liberated at an electrode is directly proportional to the quantity of electricity".

The above statement is associated with

(a) Newton's law

(b) Faraday's law of electromagnetic

(c) <u>Faraday's law of electrolysis</u>

(d) Gauss's law

2. The charge required to liberate one gram equivalent of any substance is known as _______ constant

(a) time

(b) <u>Faraday's</u>

(c) Boltzman

3. During the charging of a lead-acid cell

(a) <u>its voltage increases</u>

(b) it gives out energy

(c) its cathode becomes dark chocolate brown in colour

(d) specific gravity of H2SO4 decreases

4. The capacity of a lead-acid cell does not depend on its

(a) temperature

(b) <u>rate of charge</u>

(c) rate of discharge

(d) quantity of active material

5. During charging the specific gravity of the electrolyte of a lead-acid battery

(a) <u>increases</u>

(b) decreases

(c) remains the same

(d) becomes zero

6. The active materials on the positive and negative plates of a fully charged leadacid battery are

(a) lead and lead peroxide

(b) lead sulphate and lead

(c) lead peroxide and lead

(d) none of the above

7. When a lead-acid battery is in fully charged condition, the colour of its positive

plate is

(a) dark grey

(b) brown

(c) dark brown

(d) none of above

8. The active materials of a nickel-iron battery are

(a) nickel hydroxide

(6) powdered iron and its oxide

(c) 21% solution of KOH

(d) all of the above

9. The ratio of ampere-hour efficiency to watt-hour efficiency of a lead-acid cell is

(a) just one

(b) always greater than one

(c) always less than one

(d) none of the above.

10. The best indication about the state of charge on a lead-acid battery is given by

(a) output voltage

(b) temperature of electrolyte

(c) specific gravity of electrolyte

(d) none of the above

11. The storage battery generally used in electric power station is

(a) nickel-cadmium battery

(b) zinc-carbon battery

(c) lead-acid battery

(d) none of the above

12. The output voltage of a charger is

(a) less than the battery voltage

(b) higher than the battery voltage
(c) the same as the battery voltage
(d) none of the above
13. Cells are connected in series in order to
(a) increase the voltage rating
(6) increase the current rating
(c) increase the life of the cells
(d) none of the above
14. Five 2 V cells are connected in parallel. The output voltage is
(a) 1 V
(6) 1.5 V
(c) 1.75 V
(d) 2 V
15. The capacity of a battery is expressed in terms of
(a) current rating
(b) voltage rating
(c) ampere-hour rating
(d) none of the above
16. Duringthe charging and discharging of a nickel-iron cell
(a) corrosive fumes are produced
(b) water is neither formed nor absorbed
(c) nickel hydroxide remains unsplit
(d) its e.m.f. remains constant

17. As compared to constant-current system, the constant-voltage system of charging a lead acid cell has the advantage of

(a) reducing time of charging
(b) increasing cell capacity
(c) both (a) and (b)
(d) avoiding excessive gassing
18. A dead storage battery can be revived by
(a) adding distilled water
(6) adding so-called battery restorer
(c) a dose of H2SO4
(d) none of the above

19. As compared to a lead-acid cell, the efficiency of a nickel-iron cell is less due to its

(a) compactness
(b) lower e.m.f.

(c) small quantity of electrolyte used

(d) higher internal resistance

20. Trickle charging of a storage battery helps to

(a) maintain proper electrolyte level

(b) increase its reserve capacity

(c) prevent sulphation

(d) keep it fresh and fully charged

21. Those substances of the cell which take active part in chemical combination and hence produce electricity during charging or discharging are known as_______materials.

(a) passive

(b) active

(c) redundant

(d) inert

22. In a lead-acid cell dilute sulphuric acid (electrolyte) approximately comprises the following

(a) one part H_2O, three parts H_2SO_4

(b) two parts H_2O, two parts H_2SO_4

(c) three parts H_2O, one part H_2SO_4

(d) all H_2SO_4

23. It is noticed that durum charging

(a) there is a rise in voltage

(b) energy is absorbed by the cell

(c) specific gravity of H_2SO_4 is increased

(d) all of the above

24. It is noticed that during discharging the following does not happen

(a) both anode and cathode become $PbSO_4$

(b) specific gravity of H_2SO_4 decreases

(c) voltage of the cell decreases

(d) the cell absorbs energy

25. The ampere-hour efficiency of a leadacid cell is normally between

(a) 20 to 30%

(b) 40 to 50%

(c) 60 to 70%

(d) 90 to 95%

26. The watt-hour efficiency of a lead-acid cell varies between

(a) 25 to 35%

(b) 40 to 60%

(c) 70 to 80%
(d) 90 to 95%
27. The capacity of a lead-acid cell is measured in
(a) amperes
(b) ampere-hours
(c) watts
(d) watt-hours
28. The capacity of a lead-acid cell depends on
(a) rate of discharge
(b) temperature
(c) density of electrolyte
(d) all above
29. When the lead-acid cell is fully charged, the electrolyte assumes ______appearance
(a) dull
(b) reddish
(c) bright
(d) milky
30. The e.m.f. of an Edison cell, when fully charged, is nearly
(a) 1.4 V
(b) 1 V
(c) 0.9 V
(d) 0.8 V
31. The internal resistance of an alkali cell is nearly ______ times that of the leadacid cell.
(a) two
(b) three
(c) four
(d) five
32. The average charging voltage for alkali cell is about
(a) 1 V
(b) 1.2 V
(c) 1.7 V
(d) 2.1 V
33. On the average the ampere-hour efficiency of an Edison cell is about
(a) 40%
(b) 60%
(c) 70%

(d) 80%

34. The active material of the positive plates of silver-zinc batteries is

(a) silver oxide

(b) lead oxide

(c) lead

(d) zinc powder

35. Lead-acid cell has a life of nearly charges and discharges

(a) 500

(b) 700

(c) 1000

(d) 1250

36. Life of the Edison cell is at least

(a) five years

(b) seven years

(c) eight years

(d) ten years

37. The internal resistance of a lead-acid cell is that of Edison cell

(a) less than

(b) more than

(c) equal to

(d) none of the above

38. Electrolyte used in an Edison cell is

(a) NaOH

(b) KOH

(c) HC1

(d) HN03

39. Electrolyte used in a lead-acid cell is

(a) NaOH

(b) onlyH2S04

(c) only water

(d) dilute H2SO4

40. Negative plate of an Edison cell is made of

(a) copper

(b) lead

(c) iron

(d) silver oxide

41. The open circuit voltage of any storage cell depends wholly upon

(a) its chemical constituents

(b) on the strength of its electrolyte
(c) its temperature
(d) all above
42. The specific gravity of electrolyte is measured by
(a) manometer
(6) a mechanical gauge
(c) hydrometer
(d) psychrometer
43. When the specific gravity of the electrolyte of a lead-acid cell is reduced to 1.1 to 1.15 the cell is in
(a) charged state
(b) discharged state
(c) both (a) and (b)
(d) active state
44. In _______ system the charging current is intermittently controlled at either a
maximum or minimum value
(a) two rate charge control
(b) trickle charge
(c) floating charge
(d) an equalizing charge
45. Over charging
(a) produces excessive gassing
(b) loosens the active material
(e) increases the temperature resulting in buckling of plates
(d) all above
46. Undercharging
(a) reduces specific gravity of the electrolyte
(b) increases specific gravity of the electrolyte
(c) produces excessive gassing
(d) increases the temperature
47. Internal short circuits are caused by
(a) breakdown of one or more separators
(b) excess accumulation of sediment at the bottom of the cell
(c) both (a) and (b)
(d) none of the above
48. The effect of sulphation is that the internal resistance
(a) increases

(b) decreases

(c) remains same

(d) none of the above

49. Excessive formation of lead sulphate on the surface of the plates happens because of

(a) allowing a battery to stand in discharged condition for a long time

(b) topping up with electrolyte

(c) persistent undercharging

(d) all above

50. The substances which combine together to store electrical energy during the charge are called _______ materials

(a) active

(b) passive

(c) inert

(d) dielectric

1. The property of coil by which a counter e.m.f. is induced in it when the current

through the coil changes is known as

(a) self-inductance

(b) mutual inductance

(c) series aiding inductance

(d) capacitance

2. As per Faraday's laws of electromagnetic induction, an e.m.f. is induced in a

conductor whenever it

(a) lies perpendicular to the magnetic flux

(b) lies in a magnetic field

(c) cuts magnetic flux

(d) moves parallel to the direction of the magnetic field

3. Which of the following circuit element stores energy in the electromagnetic

field ?

(a) Inductance

(b) Condenser

(c) Variable resistor

(d) Resistance

4. The inductance of a coil will increase under all the following conditions except

(a) when more length for the same number of turns is provided
(6) when the number of turns of the coil increase
(c) when more area for each turn is provided
(d) when permeability of the core increases

5. Higher the self-inductance of a coil,
(a) lesser its weber-turns
(b) lower the e.m.f. induced
(c) greater the flux produced by it
(d) longer the delay in establishing steady current through it

6. In an iron cored coil the iron core is removed so that the coil becomes an air cored coil. The inductance of the coil will
(a) increase
(b) decrease
(c) remain the same
(d) initially increase and then decrease

7. An open coil has
(a) zero resistance and inductance
(b) infinite resistance and zero inductance
(c) infinite resistance and normal inductance
(d) zero resistance and high inductance

8. Both the number of turns and the core length of an inductive coil are doubled.
Its self-inductance will be
(a) unaffected
(b) doubled
(c) halved
(d) quadrupled

9. If current in a conductor increases then according to Lenz's law self-induced
voltage will
(a) aid the increasing current
(b) tend to decrease the amount of cur-rent
(c) produce current opposite to the in-creasing current
(d) aid the applied voltage

10. The direction of induced e.m.f. can be found by
(a) Laplace's law
(b) Lenz's law
(c) Fleming's right hand rule

(d) Kirchhoff s voltage law

11. Air-core coils are practically free from

(a) hysteresis losses

(b) eddy current losses

(c) both (a) and (b)

(d) none of the above

12. The magnitude of the induced e.m.f. in a conductor depends on the

(a) flux density of the magnetic field

(b) amount of flux cut

(c) amount of flux linkages

(d) rate of change of flux-linkages

13. Mutually inductance between two magnetically-coupled coils depends on

(a) permeability of the core

(b) the number of their turns

(c) cross-sectional area of their common core

(d) all of the above

14. A laminated iron core has reduced eddy-current losses because

(a) more wire can be used with less D.C. resistance in coil

(b) the laminations are insulated from each other

(c) the magnetic flux is concentrated in the air gap of the core

(d) the laminations are stacked vertfcally

15. The law that the induced e.m.f. and current always oppose the cause producing them is due to

(a) Faraday

(b) Lenz

(c) Newton

16. Which of the following is not a unit of inductance ?

(a) Henry

(b) Coulomb/volt ampere

(c) Volt second per ampere

(d) All of the above

17. In case of an inductance, current is proportional to

(a) voltage across the inductance

(b) magnetic field

(c) both (a) and (b)

(d) neither (a) nor (b)

18. Which of the following circuit elements will oppose the change in circuit

current ?

(a) Capacitance

(b) Inductance

(c) Resistance

(d) All of the above

19. For a purely inductive circuit which of the following is true ?

(a) Apparent power is zero

(b) Relative power is.zero

(c) Actual power of the circuit is zero

(d) Any capacitance even if present in the circuit will not be charged

20. Which of the following is unit of inductance ?

(a) Ohm

(b) Henry

(c) Ampere turns

(d) Webers/metre

21. An e.m.f. of 16 volts is induced in a coil of inductance 4H. The rate of change

of current must be

(a) 64 A/s

(b) 32 A/s

(c) 16 A/s

(d) 4 A/s

22. The core of a coil has a length of 200 mm. The inductance of coil is 6 mH. If

the core length is doubled, all other quantities, remaining the same, the inductance will be

(a) 3 mH

(b) 12 mH

(c) 24mH

(d)48mH

23. The self inductances of two coils are 8 mH and 18 mH. If the co-efficients of

coupling is 0.5, the mutual inductance of the coils is

(a) 4 mH

(b) 5 mH

(c) 6 mH

(d) 12 mH

24. Two coils have inductances of 8 mH and 18 mH and a co-efficient of coupling

of 0.5. If the two coils are connected in series aiding, the total inductance will be

(a) 32 mH

(b) 38 mH

(c) 40 mH

(d) 48 mH

25. A 200 turn coil has an inductance of 12 mH. If the number of turns is

increased to 400 turns, all other quantities (area, length etc.) remaining the same,

the inductance will be

(a) 6 mH

(b) 14 mH

(c) 24 mH

(d) 48 mH

26. Two coils have self-inductances of 10 H and 2 H, the mutual inductance being

zero. If the two coils are connected in series, the total inductance will be

(a) 6 H

(b) 8 H

(c) 12 H

(d) 24 H

27. In case all the flux from the current in coil 1 links with coil 2, the co-efficient

of coupling will be

(a) 2.0

(b) 1.0

(c) 0.5

(d) zero

28. A coil with negligible resistance has 50V across it with 10 mA. The inductive

reactance is

(a) 50 ohms

(b) 500 ohms

(c) 1000 ohms

(d) 5000 ohms

29. A conductor 2 meters long moves at right angles to a magnetic field of flux

density 1 tesla with a velocity of 12.5 m/s. The induced e.m.f. in the conductor will

be

(a) 10 V

(6) 15 V

(c) 25V

(d) 50V

30. Lenz's law is a consequence of the law of conservation of

(a) induced current

(b) charge

(c) energy

(d) induced e.m.f.

31. A conductor carries 125 amperes of current under 60° to a magnetic field of 1.1

tesla. The force on the conductor will be

nearly

(a) 50 N

(b) 120 N

(c) 240 N

(d) 480 N

32. Find the force acting on a conductor 3m long carrying a current of 50 amperes

at right angles to a magnetic field having a flux density of 0.67 tesla.

(a) 100 N

(b) 400 N

(c) 600 N

(d) 1000 N

33. The co-efficient of coupling between two air core coils depends on

(a) self-inductance of two coils only

(b) mutual inductance between two coils only

(c) mutual inductance and self inductance of two coils

(d) none of the above

34. An average voltage of 10 V is induced in a 250 turns solenoid as a result of a

change in flux which occurs in 0.5 second. The total flux change is

(a) 20 Wb
(b) 2 Wb
(c) 0.2 Wb
(d) 0.02 Wb

35. A 500 turns solenoid develops an average induced voltage of 60 V. Over what
time interval must a flux change of 0.06 Wb occur to produce such a voltage ?
(a) 0.01 s
(b) 0.1 s
(c) 0.5 s
(d) 5 s

36. Which of the fpllowing inductor will have the least eddy current losses ?
(a) Air core
(b) Laminated iron core
(c) Iron core
(d) Powdered iron core

37. A coil induces 350 mV when the current changes at the rate of 1 A/ s. The
value of inductance is
(a) 3500 mH
(b) 350 mH
(c) 250 mH
(d) 150 mH

38. Two 300 uH coils in series without mutual coupling have a total inductance of
(a) 300 uH
(b) 600 uH
(c) 150 uH
(d) 75 uH

39. Current changing from 8 A to 12 A in one second induced 20 volts in a coil.
The value of inductance is
(a) 5 mH
(b) 10 mH
(c) 5 H
(d) 10 H

40. Which circuit element(s) will oppose the change in circuit current ?
(a) Resistance only
(b) Inductance only
(c) Capacitance only
(d) Inductance and capacitance
41. A crack in the magnetic path of an inductor will result in
(a) unchanged inductance
(b) increased inductance
(c) zero inductance
(d) reduced inductance
42. A coil is wound on iron core which carries current I. The self-induced voltage
in the coil is not affected by
(a) variation in coil current
(b) variation in voltage to the coil
(c) change of number of turns of coil
(d) the resistance of magnetic path
1. A semiconductor is formed by .... bonds.
A] Covalent
B] Electrovalent
C] Co-ordinate
D] None of the above
2. A semiconductor has .... temperature coefficient of resistance.
A] Positive
B] Zero
C] Negative
D] None of the above
3. The most commonly used semiconductor is ....
A] Germanium
B] Silicon
C] Carbon
D] Sulphur
6. The resistivity of a pure silicon is about ....
A] 100 O cm
B] 6000 O cm
C] 3 x 105 O m
D] 6 x 10-8 O cm
7. When a pure semiconductor is heated, its resistance ....

A] Goes up

B] Goes down

C] Remains the same

D] Can't say

8. The strength of a semiconductor crystal comes from ....

A] Forces between nuclei

B] Forces between protons

C] Electron-pair bonds

D] None of the above

9. When a pentavalent impurity is added to a pure semiconductor, it becomes ....

A] An insulator

B] An intrinsic semiconductor

C] p-type semiconductor

D] n-type semiconductor

10. Addition of pentavalent impurity to a semiconductor createsmany ....

A] Free electrons

B] Holes

C] Valence electrons

D] Bound electrons

11. A pentavalent impurity has .... Valence electrons

A] 35

B] 4

C] 6

12. An n-type semiconductor is ....

A] Positively charged

B] Negatively charged

C] Electrically neutral

D] None of the above

14. Addition of trivalent impurity to a semiconductor creates many ....

A] Holes

B] Free electrons

C] Valence electrons

D] Bound electrons

15. A hole in a semiconductor is defined as ....

A] A free electron

B] The incomplete part of an electron pair bond

C] A free proton

D] A free neutron

16. The impurity level in an extrinsic semiconductor is about ..... of pure semiconductor.

A] 10 atoms for 108 atoms

B] 1 atom for 108 atoms

C] 1 atom for 104 atoms

D] 1 atom for 100 atoms

17. As the doping to a pure semiconductor increases, the bulk resistance of the semiconductor ....

A] Remains the same

B] Increases

C] Decreases

D] None of the above

18. A hole and electron in close proximity would tend to ....

A] Repel each other

B] Attract each other

C] Have no effect on each other

D] None of the above

19. In a semiconductor, current conduction is due to ....

A] Only holes

B] Only free electrons

C] Holes and free electrons

D] None of the above

20. The random motion of holes and free electrons due to thermal agitation is called ....

A] Diffusion

B] Pressure

C] Ionisation

D] None of the above

21. A forward biased pn junction diode has a resistance of the order of

A] Ok

B] O

C] MO

D] None of the above

22. The battery connections required to forward bias a pn junction are ......

A] +ve terminal to p and –ve terminal to n

B] -ve terminal to p and +ve terminal to n
C] -ve terminal to p and –ve terminal to n
D] None of the above
23. The barrier voltage at a pn junction for germanium is about ....
A] 5 V
B] 3 V
C] Zero
D] 3 V
24. In the depletion region of a pn junction, there is a shortage of ....
A] Acceptor ions
B] Holes and electrons
C] Donor ions
D] None of the above
25. A reverse bias pn junction has ....
A] narrow depletion layer
B] Almost no current
C] Very low resistance
D] Large current flow
26. A pn junction acts as a ....
A] Controlled switch
B] Bidirectional switch
C] Unidirectional switch
D] None of the above
27. A reverse biased pn junction has resistance of the order of
A] Ok
B] O
C] MO
D] None of the above
28. The leakage current across a pn junction is due to ....
A] Minority carriers
B] Majority carriers
C] Junction capacitance
D] None of the above
29. When the temperature of an extrinsic semiconductor is increased, the pronounced effect is on......
A] Junction capacitance
B] Minority carriers
C] Majority carriers

D] None of the above

30. With forward bias to a pn junction , the width of depletion layer ....

A] Decreases

B] Increases

C] Remains the same

D] None of the above

31. The leakage current in a pn junction is of the order of

A] Aa

B] mA

C] kA

D] µA

32. In an intrinsic semiconductor, the number of free electrons ....

A] Equals the number of holes

B] Is greater than the number of holes

C] Is less than the number of holes

D] None of the above

33. At room temperature, an intrinsic semiconductor has ....

A] Many holes only

B] A few free electrons and holes

C] Many free electrons only

D] No holes or free electrons

34. At absolute temperature, an intrinsic semiconductor has ....

A] A few free electrons

B] Many holes

C] Many free electrons

D] No holes or free electrons

35. At room temperature, an intrinsic silicon crystal acts approximately as ......

A] A battery

B] A conductor

C] An insulator

D] A piece of copper wire

1. A crystal diode has ....

one pn junction

two pn junctions

three pn junctions

none of the above

ANS: 1

2. A crystal diode has forward resistance of the order of ....

kΩ

Ω

MΩ

none of the above

ANS: 2

3. If the arrow of crystal diode symbol is positive w.r.t. bar, then diode is .... biased.

forward

reverse

either forward or reverse

none of the above

ANS: 1

SEMICONDUCTOR DIODE

Questions and Answers pdf

4. The reverse current in a diode is of the order of ....

kA

mA

μA

A

ANS: 3

5. The forward voltage drop across a silicon diode is about ....

2.5 V

3 V

10 V

0.7 V

ANS: 4

6. A crystal diode is used as ....

an amplifier

a rectifier

an oscillator

a voltage regulator

ANS: 2

7. The d.c. resistance of a crystal diode is .... its a.c. resistance

the same as

more than

less than
none of the above
ANS: 3
8. An ideal crystal diode is one which behaves as a perfect .... when forward biased.
conductor
insulator
resistance material
none of the above
ANS: 1
9. The ratio of reverse resistance and forward resistance of a germanium crystal diode is about ....
1 : 1
100 : 1
1000 : 1
40,000 : 1
ANS: 4
10. The leakage current in a crystal diode is due to ....
minority carriers
majority carriers
junction capacitance
none of the above
ANS: 1
11. If the temperature of a crystal diode increases, then leakage current ....
remains the same
decreases
increases
becomes zero
ANS: 3
12. The PIV rating of a crystal diode is .... that of equivalent vacuum diode
the same as
lower than
more than
none of the above
ANS: 2
13. If the doping level of a crystal diode is increased, the breakdown

voltage.............
remains the same
is increased
is decreased
none of the above
ANS: 3
14. The knee voltage of a crystal diode is approximately equal to ....
applied voltage
breakdown voltage
forward voltage
barrier potential
ANS: 4
15. When the graph between current through and voltage across a device is a straight line, the device is referred to as ....
linear
active
nonlinear
passive
ANS: 1
16. When the crystal current diode current is large, the bias is ....
forward
inverse
poor
reverse
ANS: 1
17. A crystal diode is a .... device
non-linear
bilateral
linear
none of the above
ANS: 1
18. A crystal diode utilises .... characteristic for rectification
reverse
forward
forward or reverse
none of the above
ANS: 2

19. When a crystal diode is used as a rectifier, the most important consideration is ....
forward characteristic
doping level
reverse characteristic
PIC rating
ANS: 4
20. If the doping level in a crystal diode is increased, the width of depletion layer...........
remains the same
is decreased
in increased
none of the above
ANS: 3
21. A zener diode has ....
one pn junction
two pn junctions
three pn junctions
none of the above
ANS: 1
22. A zener diode is used as ....
an amplifier
a voltage regulator
a rectifier
a multivibrator
ANS: 2
23. The doping level in a zener diode is .... that of a crystal diode
the same as
less than
more than
none of the above
ANS: 3
24. A zener diode is always .... connected.
reverse
forward
either reverse or forward
none of the above
ANS: 1

25. A zener diode utilizes .... characteristics for its operation.
forward
reverse
both forward and reverse
none of the above
ANS: 2
26. In the breakdown region, a zener didoe behaves like a .... source.
constant voltage
constant current
constant resistance
none of the above
ANS: 1
27. A zener diode is destroyed if it..............
is forward biased
is reverse biased
carrier more than rated current
none of the above
ANS: 3
28. A series resistance is connected in the zener circuit to...........
properly reverse bias the zener
protect the zener
properly forward bias the zener
none of the above
ANS: 2
29. A zener diode is .... device
a non-linear
a linear
an amplifying
none of the above
ANS: 1
30. A zener diode has .... breakdown voltage
undefined
sharp
zero
none of the above
ANS: 2
31. .... rectifier has the lowest forward resistance

solid state
vacuum tube
gas tube
none of the above
ANS: 1
32. Mains a.c. power is converrted into d.c. power for ....
lighting purposes
heaters
using in electronic equipment
none of the above
ANS: 3
33. The disadvantage of a half-wave rectifier is that the..................
components are expensive
diodes must have a higher power rating
output is difficult to filter
none of the above
ANS: 3
34. If the a.c. input to a half-wave rectifier is an r.m.s value of 400/√2 volts, then diode PIV rating is ....
400/√2 V
400 V
400 x √2 V
none of the above
ANS: 2
35. The ripple factor of a half-wave rectifier is ....
21
.21
2.5
0.48
ANS: 4
36. There is a need of transformer for ....
half-wave rectifier
centre-tap full-wave rectifier
bridge full-wave rectifier
none of the above
ANS: 2
37. The PIV rating of each diode in a bridge rectifier is .... that of the equivalent centre-tap rectifier

one-half
the same as
twice
four times
ANS: 1
38. For the same secondary voltage, the output voltage from a centretap rectifier is .... than that of bridge rectifier
twice
thrice
four time
one-half
ANS: 4
39. If the PIV rating of a diode is exceeded, ...
the diode conducts poorly
the diode is destroyed
the diode behaves like a zener diode
none of the above
ANS: 2
40. A 10 V power supply would use .... as filter capacitor.
paper capacitor
mica capacitor
electrolytic capacitor
air capacitor
ANS: 3
41. A 1,000 V power supply would use .... as a filter capacitor
paper capacitor
air capacitor
mica capacitor
electrolytic capacitor
ANS: 1
42. The .... filter circuit results in the best voltage regulation
choke input
capacitor input
resistance input
none of the above
ANS: 1
43. A half-wave rectifier has an input voltage of 240 V r.m.s. If the step-down transformer has a turns ratio of 8:1, what is the peak load

voltage? Ignore diode drop.

27.5 V

86.5 V

30 V

42.5 V

ANS: 4

44. The maximum efficiency of a half-wave rectifier is ....

40.6 %

81.2 %

50 %

25 %

ANS: 1

45. The most widely used rectifier is ....

half-wave rectifier

centre-tap full-wave rectifier

bridge full-wave rectifier

none of the above

ANS:3

1. A transistor has ....

A] one pn junction

B] <u>two pn junctions</u>

C] three pn junctions

D] four pn junctions

2. The number of depletion layers in a transistor is ....

A] four

B] three

C] one

D] <u>two</u>

3. The base of a transistor is .... doped

A] heavily

B] moderately

C] <u>lightly</u>

D] none of the above

4. The element that has the biggest size in a transistor is ....

A] <u>collector</u>

B] base

C] emitter

D] collector-base-junction

5. In a pnp transistor, the current carriers are ....
A] acceptor ions
B] donor ions
C] free electrons
D] holes
6. The collector of a transistor is .... doped
A] heavily
B] moderately
C] lightly
D] none of the above
7. A transistor is a .... operated device
A] current
B] voltage
C] both voltage and current
D] none of the above
8. In a npn transistor, ... are the minority carriers
A] free electrons
B] holes
C] donor ions
D] acceptor ions
9. The emitter of a transistor is .... doped
A] lightly
B] heavily
C] moderately
D] none of the above
10. In a transistor, the base current is about .... of emitter current
A] 25%
B] 20%
C] 35 %
D] 5%
11. At the base-emitter junctions of a transistor, one finds ....
A] a reverse bias
B] a wide depletion layer
C] low resistance
D] none of the above
12. The input impedance of a transistor is ....
A] high
B] low

C] very high
D] almost zero
13. Most of the majority carriers from the emitter ....
A] recombine in the base
B] recombine in the emitter
C] pass through the base region to the collector
D] none of the above
14. The current IB is ....
A] electron current
B] hole current
C] donor ion current
D] acceptor ion current
15. In a transistor ....
A] IC = IE + IB
B] IB = IC + IE
C] IE = IC – IB
D] IE = IC + IB
16. The value of a of a transistor is ....
A] more than 1
B] less than 1
C] 1
D] none of the above
17. IC = aIE + ...
A] IB
B] ICEO
C] ICBO
D] ßIB
18. The output impedance of a transistor is ....
A] high
B] zero
C] low
D] very low
19. In a tansistor, IC = 100 mA and IE = 100.2 mA. The value of ß is ....
A] 100
B] 50
C] about 1
D] 200

20. In a transistor if ß = 100 and collector current is 10 mA, then IE is ....

A] 100 mA

B] <u>100.1 mA</u>

C] 110 mA

D] none of the above

21. The relation between ß and a is ....

A] ß = 1 / (1 – a)

B] ß = (1 – a) / a

C] <u>ß = a / (1 – a)</u>

D] ß = a / (1 + a)

22. The value of ß for a transistor is generally ....

A] 1less than 1

B] between 20 and 500

C] <u>above 500</u>

23. The most commonly used transistor arrangement is .... arrangement

A] <u>common emitter</u>

B] common base

C] common collector

D] none of the above

24. The input impedance of a transistor connected in ....arrangement is the highest

A] common emitter

B] <u>common collector</u>

C] common base

D] none of the above

25. The output impedance of a transistor connected in ....

A] arrangement is the highest

B] common emitter

C] <u>common collector</u>

D] common base

none of the above

26. The phase difference between the input and output voltages in a common base arrangement is ....

A] 180o

B] 90o

C] 270o

D] <u>0o</u>

27. The power gain in a transistor connected in .... arrangement is the highest

A] common emitter

B] common base

C] common collector

D] none of the above

28. The phase difference between the input and output voltages of a transistor connected in common emitter arrangement is ....

A] 0o

B] 180o

C] 90o

D] 270o

29. The voltage gain in a transistor connected in .... arrangement is the highest

A] common base

B] common collector

C] common emitter

D] none of the above

30. As the temperature of a transistor goes up, the base-emitter resistance ....

A] decreases

B] increases

C] remains the same

D] none of the above

31. The voltage gain of a transistor connected in common collector

A] arrangement is ....

B] equal to 1

C] more than 10

D] more than 100 less than 1

32. The phase difference between the input and output voltages of a transistor connected in common collector arrangement is ....

A] 180o

B] 0o

C] 90o

D] 270o

33. IC = ß IB + ...

A] ICBO

B] IC
C] ICEO
D] aIE
34. IC = [a / (1 – a)] IB + ...
A] ICEO
B] ICBO
C] IC
D] (1 – a) IB
35. IC = [a / (1 – a)] IB + [........ / (1 – a)]
A] ICBO
B] ICEO
C] IC
D] IE
36. BC 147 transistor indicates that it is made of ....
A] germanium
B] silicon
C] carbon
D] none of the above
37. ICEO = (.........) ICBO
A] ß1
B] + a
C] 1 + ß
D] none of the above
38. A transistor is connected in CB mode. If it is not connected in CE mode with same bias voltages, the values of IE, IB and IC will ....
A] remain the same
B] increase
C] decrease
D] none of the above
39. If the value of a is 0.9, then value of ß is ....
A] 9
B] 0.9
C] 900
D] 90
40. In a transistor, signal is transferred from a .... circuit
A] high resistance to low resistance
B] low resistance to high resistance
C] high resistance to high resistance

D] low resistance to low resistance

41. The arrow in the symbol of a transistor indicates the direction of ....

A] electron current in the emitter

B] electron current in the collector

C] hole current in the emitter

D] donor ion current

42. The leakage current in CE arrangement is .... that in CB arrangement

A] more than

B] less than

C] the same as

D] none of the above

43. A heat sink is generally used with a transistor to ....

A] increase the forward current

B] decrease the forward current

C] compensate for excessive doping

D] prevent excessive temperature rise

44. The most commonly used semiconductor in the manufacture of a transistor is ....

A] germanium

B] silicon

C] carbon

D] none of the above

45. The collector-base junction in a transistor has ....

A] forward bias at all times

B] reverse bias at all times

C] low resistance

D] none of the above

1) Which fluid is used in hydraulic power systems?

a] water

b] oil

c] non-compressible fluid

d] all of the above

2) Pressure of 1 bar is equal to

a] 14]5 psi

b] 145 psi

c] 12]5 psi

d] 145 x 10-6 psi

4) What effect does overloading have on fluid power and electrical systems?

a] electrical components get damaged in electrical systems

b] fluid power system stops working without damaging the components

c] both a] and b]

d] none of the above

5) How is power transmitted in fluid power systems?

a] power is transmitted instantaneously

b] power is transmitted gradually

c] both a] and b]

d] none of the above

6) Generally liquids are non-compressible but when a large pressure of 70 bar is applied, petroleum oil can be compressed up to

a] 0]5% of its original volume

b] 1% of its original volume

c] 5% of its original volume

d] none of the above

8) The resistance offered to the flow of fluid inside a piston develops into

a] pressure

b] force

c] stress

d] all of the above

9) At low pressures, liquids are

a] compressible

b] non-compressible

c] unpredictable

11) In hydraulic systems,

a] the mechanical energy is transferred to the oil and then converted into mechanical energy

b] the electrical energy is transferred to the oil and then converted into mechanical energy

c] the mechanical energy is transferred to the oil and converted into electrical energy

d] none of the above

12) Which of the following is used as a component in hydraulic power unit?

a] pressure gauge

b] filler gauge
c] valve
d] reservoir
13) Rotary motion in a hydraulic power unit is achieved by using
a] hydraulic cylinder
b] pneumatic cylinder
c] both hydraulic and pneumatic cylinder
d] none of the above
16) What is the relation between speed and flow rate for fixed displacement vane pump?
a] flow rate increases with increase in speed of rotor
b] flow rate decreases with increase in speed of rotor
c] flow rate is constant and does not change with change in speed
d] none of the above
17) In fixed displacement vane pump,
a] flow rate decreases with increase in working pressure
b] flow rate increases with increase in working pressure
c] flow rate is constant and does not change with working pressure
d] none of the above
18) Which type of motion is transmitted by hydraulic actuators?
a] linear motion
b] rotary motion
c] both a] and b]
d] none of the above
19) What is the function of electric actuator?
a] converts electrical energy into mechanical torque
b] converts mechanical torque into electrical energy
c] converts mechanical energy into mechanical torque
d] none of the above
20) Which of the following is a hydraulic cylinder based on construction?
a] single acting cylinder
b] double acting cylinder
c] welded design cylinder
d] all of the above
21) Which energy is converted into mechanical energy by the hydraulic cylinders?
a] hydrostatic energy

b] hydrodynamic energy
c] electrical energy
d] none of the above
22) What is the advantage of using a single acting cylinder?
a] high cost and reliable
b] honing inside the inner surface of pump is not required
c] piston seals are not required
d] all of the above
23) What is the function of a flow control valve?
a] flow control valve changes the direction of oil flow
b] flow control valve can adjust the flow rate of hydraulic oil
c] both a] and b]
d] none of the above
24) What does the numbers in 4/2 valve mean?
a] 4 positions and 2 ways
b] 4 ways and 2 positions
c] none of the above
d] 3 ways 2 positions
25) Which type of solenoid has more chances of coil failure?
a] AC solenoid
b] DC solenoid
c] both AC and DC solenoids
d] none of the above
26) Which stage in two stage direction control valve is solenoid operated?
a] main stage direction control valve
b] pilot stage direction control valve
c] both stages in two stage direction control are solenoid operated
d] none of the above
28) Which of the following is a gas charged accumulator?
a] bladder type
b] spring loaded accumulator
c] weighted accumulator
d] all of the above
29) How is pressure of fluid under piston calculated in a weighted accumulator?
a] pressure of fluid = (weight added / piston area)
b] pressure of fluid = (piston area / weight added)

c] pressure of fluid = (weight added / piston force)
d] pressure of fluid = (piston force / weight added)
30) Which of the following gas is used in gas charged accumulator?
a] oxygen
b] <u>nitrogen</u>
c] carbon dioxide
d] all of the above
31) The relation for rapid change in pressure and volume adiabatically is given as
a] p0 v0 = p1 v1 = p2 v2
b] p0 v0 = p1 v1n = p2 v2n
c] <u>p0 v0n = p1 v1n = p2 v2n</u>
d] none of the above
32) Why is the pilot operated check valve used in clamping operation?
a] to reduce leakage in spool valve
b] to avoid decrease in pressure during clamping
c] <u>*both a] and b*</u>]
d] none of the above
33) Which area does the part shown below indicate?
a] rod area
b] full bore area
c] <u>annulus area</u>
d] none of the above
34) Which of the following statements is true?
a] Meter-in feed circuits have speed control in two directions
b] <u>Standard block feed circuits have speed control in two directions</u>
c] Tank line feed control systems have speed control only in one direction
d] all of the above
35) Leakage in rotary chucks can be compensated by
a] flow control valve
b] pilot operated check valve
c] <u>accumulator</u>
d] all of the above
36) Which valve is used to block the accumulator from the system for the purpose of safety?
a] pilot valve
b] <u>needle valve</u>

c] detent valve
d] all of the above

37) Which of the following systems generate more energy when used in industrial applications?
a] hydraulic systems
b] pneumatic systems
c] both systems generate same energy
d] cannot say

38) Which type of compressor requires a reservoir for compressed air and why?
a] rotary compressor to avoid pulsating effect
b] reciprocating compressor to avoid pulsating effect
c] both rotary and reciprocating compressors to avoid pulsating effect
d] none of the above

39) Which of the following factors is/are considered while selecting a compressor?
a] type of oil filter required
b] volumetric efficiency
c] viscosity of the liquids used
d] all of the above

40) Which of the following is a component used in air generation system?
a] pressure switch
b] pressure gauge
c] drier
d] intercooler

41) Where is an intercooler connected in a two stage compressor?
a] intercooler is connected after the two stage compressor
b] intercooler is connected between the two stages of the compressor
c] intercooler is connected before the two stage compressor
d] none of the above

43) Which of the following notations is used to represent a regulator unit?
a] 3]0
b] 0]3
c] 3
d] none of the above

44) Which of the following logic valve is known as shuttle valve?

a] OR gate
b] AND gate
c] NOR gate
d] NAND

45) In pneumatic systems, AND gate is also known as
a] check valve
b] shuttle valve
c] dual pressure valve
d] none of the above

46) What is a pressure sequence valve?
a] it is a combination of adjustable pressure relief valve and directional control valve
b] it is a combination of nonadjustable pressure relief valve and directional control valve
c] it is a combination of adjustable pressure reducing valve and check valve
d] it is a combination of adjustable pressure reducing valve and flow control valve

47) Overlapping of signals in pneumatic systems can be avoided by using
a] rolling lever valve
b] idle roller lever valve
c] both a] and b]
d] none of the above

49) Which of the following statements is true for cascade method which is used to draw a pneumatic circuit?
a] signal processing valves are connected in parallel
b] when the number of signal processing valves are greater than 4, the signals are strong
c] cascade method does not consider the cost factor
d] all of the above

50) What is the part, shown in below diagram of 3/2 valve, called?
a] manually operated valve
b] pilot operated valve
c] pressure electric converter
d] none of the above

1) In which systems, spool of the servo valve is operated by a torque motor?
a] hydromechanical servo systems

b] electrohydraulic servo systems

c] conventional servo valve

d] all of the above

2) What does servo mean in servo valve system?

a] it cannot receive a feedback but the desired output can be obtained

b] it cannot receive a feedback and the desired output cannot be obtained

c] it can receive a feedback and the desired output can be obtained

d] none of the above

3) In conventional valves, which component is used to move the spool?

a] torque motor

b] mechanical servo valve

c] solenoid

d] all of the above

4) What is the advantage of DC solenoid coils?

a] DC solenoid coils have high rush in current

b] DC solenoid coils have constant level of current

c] DC solenoid coils have rating of 220 V DC

d] all of the above

5) Which of the following statements is true for a proportional valve?

a] spool of the proportional valve can travel maximum length

b] digital type of functioning is possible in proportional valve

c] proportional valve requires a separate flow control valve

d] all of the above

6) Which of the following statements is/are false?

a] air is non-compressible

b] less power is developed in fluid power systems than conventional systems

c] mechanical linkages used for load handling purposes have high efficiency

d] all of the above

8) The hydraulic system is

a] less precise than pneumatic system

b] more precise than pneumatic system

c] both hydraulic and pneumatic systems are same on basis of precision

d] none of the above

9) Which energy is used to transmit power in hydrostatic system?

a] pressure energy

b] kinetic energy

c] potential energy

d] all of the above

10) Which system uses kinetic energy to transmit power?

a] hydrostatic system

b] <u>hydrodynamic system</u>

c] pneumatic system

d] none of the above

11) If no load is attached to piston rod, the movement of piston assembly is possible when

a] oil overcomes its self weight

b] oil overcomes friction in the piston rod assembly

c] <u>both a] and b]</u>

d] none of the above

13) Which factor helps in obtaining high speed of the piston rod in the hydraulic system?

a] decreased friction

b] pump capacity

c] increased flow rate

d] <u>all of the above</u>

14) During any operation in hydraulic system, oil prefers the path of

a] <u>least resistance</u>

b] maximum resistance

c] both a] and b]

d] none of the above

15) In a hydraulic circuit a pump is provided with two outlet paths, one where load is attached and other to the reservoir] Which path will the oil choose to flow first?

a] oil will flow to the path where load is attached

b] <u>oil will flow back to the reservoir first</u>

c] oil will flow through both the paths simultaneously

d] none of the above

16) Which of the following is used as an accessory in hydraulic power unit?

a] pumps

b] valves

c] motor

d] <u>reservoir</u>

17) Which type of pump is used for lifting water from the ground surface to the top of the building?

a] centrifugal pump

b] turbine pump

c] submersible pump

d] <u>all of the above</u>

18) Pumps used in hydraulic applications are

a] positive displacement pumps

b] variable displacement pumps

c] fixed displacement pumps

d] <u>all of the above</u>

19) What is a positive displacement pump?

a] oil from suction side of the pump flows completely to the delivery side

b] volume of fluid discharged cannot return back to the suction side of the pump

c] discharges fixed volume of fluid every cycle

d] <u>all of the above</u>

20) While operating a positive displacement pump,

a] the shut-off valve should be closed on delivery side

b] the shut-off valve should be closed on suction side

c] <u>the shut-off valve should be opened on delivery side</u>

d] none of the above

21) What effect does working pressure have on input power for radial piston pumps?

a] as working pressure increases input power decreases

b] <u>as working pressure increases input power increases</u>

c] pressure remains constant for different input powers

d] none of the above

22) Radial piston pumps can have,

a] cylinder block rotating and cam stationary

b] cylinder block stationary and cam rotating

c] <u>both a] and b]</u>

d] none of the above

23) Why are hydraulic cylinders cushioned?

a] cushioning decelerates the piston of a cylinder

b] stress and vibrations can be reduced

c] <u>both a] and b]</u>

d] none of the above

24) Which of the following statements is true?

a] Tie-rod cylinders are used in applications having working pressure of 70 bar

b] Welded type cylinders are used in systems having working pressure more than 70 bar

c] Tie-rod cylinders can be used in systems having working pressure more than 70 bar

d] <u>all of the above</u>

25) Which of these actions does a hydraulic cylinder perform?

a] pushing

b] lifting

c] <u>both a] and b]</u>

d] none of the above

26) Leakage in welded type of hydraulic cylinder is prevented by

a] wiper in gland cover

b] rod seal in end cover

c] <u>rod seal in gland cover</u>

d] none of the above

27)In single acting hydraulic cylinders the piston comes back to its original position due to

a] spring force

b] self-weight

c] momentum of a flywheel

d] <u>all of the above</u>

28) Check valve is a type of

a] pressure reducing valve

b] pressure relief valve

c] <u>directional control valve</u>

d] none of the above

29) A pressure relief valve can be

a] direct operated

b] pilot operated

c] solenoid operated

d] <u>all of the above</u>

31) How is reverse flow possible in pilot operated check valve?

a] spring force lifts the ball due to which reverse flow is possible

b] <u>fluid pressure lifts the ball due to which reverse flow is possible</u>

c] both a] and b]

d] none of the above

32) What is the difference between pressure relief valve and pressure reducing valve?

a] pressure reducing valve is connected between pump and tank line while pressure relief valve is connected between DCV and branch circuit

b] pressure relief valve is always normally opened

c] pressure reducing valve is connected between DCV and branch circuit while pressure relief valve is connected between pump and tank

d] none of the above

33) Accumulator used in gas charged accumulator is

a] hydraulic

b] pneumatic

c] hydropneumatic

d] none of the above

34) What is the function of pressure switch?

a] pressure switch is used to start a motor

b] pressure switch is used to stop a motor

c] pressure switch is used to de-energize a solenoid

d] all of the above

35) Intensifier used in pneumatic systems has output pressure

a] less than input pressure

b] more than input pressure

c] same as input pressure

d] none of the above

36) What is the function of unloading relief valve and can it be used as an accessory for accumulators?

a] unloading relief valve is used to charge the accumulator by a pump when accumulator pressure falls below the set value and it can be used as an accessory]

b] unloading relief valve is used to charge the accumulator by a pump when accumulator pressure falls below the set value but is not used as an accessory

c] unloading relief valve is used to charge the accumulator by a pump when accumulator pressure rises above the set value but is not used as an accessory

d] unloading relief valve is used to charge the accumulator by a pump when accumulator pressure rises above the set value and is used as an accessory

37) Cylinder has a bore area of 300 cm 2 and velocity of 180 cm/min] Calculate the flow rate of a pump

a] 55 l/min

b] 50 l/min

c] 54 l/min

d] none of the above

38) Which of the following statements is true, for two pumps used in circuit when initially fast operation is performed to reach a job and feeding operation is done at a slow speed?

a] initially to reach a job, a tool must be connected to a pump of high discharge and low pressure

b] initially to reach a job, a tool must be connected to a pump of low discharge and high pressure

c] for feeding operation low discharge low pressure pump is required

d] none of the above

39) What are different operations performed by PLC's?

a] Boolean logic

b] Timing

c] Arithmetic

d] all of the above

40) Which of the following pumps saves more power?

a] single pump

b] double pump

c] single and double pump use same amount of power

d] none of the above

41) What is the advantage of PLC?

a] easy to find errors

b] replacements can be easily made

c] PLC's are easily programmed

d] all of the above

43) Mass of water vapour in unit volume of air is known as

a] relative humidity

b] absolute humidity

c] saturation quantity

d] none of the above

44) Which valve is also known as memory valve?

a] single pilot signal valve

b] double pilot signal valve

c] roller lever valve

d] logic valve

45) What is the difference between signal air and control air?

a] signal air actuates final control valve and control air flows to the cylinder through the final control valve for forward and backward movement of piston rod

b] control air actuates final control valve and signal air flows to the cylinder through the final control valve for forward and backward movement of piston rod

c] both a] and b]

d] none of the above

46) Which of the following is used to sense the initial and final positions of a piston rod?

a] lever operated direction control valve

b] limit switch

c] roller lever valve

d] all of the above

47) Which valve gets activated only in one direction that is forward or backward movement of the piston rod?

a] roller lever valve

b] idle roller lever valve

c] both a] and b]

d] none of the above

48) Which numbers are used to denote retraction of a piston rod?

a] even numbers

b] odd numbers

c] both even and odd numbers

d] none of the above

49) Which of the following is an element of time delay valve?

a] flow control valve

b] direction control valve

c] both a] and b] d] none of the above

d] none of above

50) Which of the following is a type of cushioning in hydraulic cylinders?

a] trunnion cushioning

b] adjustable cushioning

c] clevis cushioning

d] none of the above

1) How is proximity switch differentiated from limit switch?

a] proximity switch is activated when moving parts have physical contact with it

b] proximity switch is activated when non-moving parts have physical contact

c] proximity switch is activated when moving parts are close to it

d] none of the above

2) Which of the following statements is true?

a] electromagnetic relays have high reliability at more cost

b] electromagnetic relays use low current and voltage, to have open or close contact in high voltage and current circuit

c] air pressure passed to pressure electric converter opens a contact which energizes a circuit for the flow of electric contact

d] all of the above

3) In which circuits, relay of low voltage and low current is used to make open or close contact?

a] high voltage and high current circuit

b] low voltage and low current circuit

c] high voltage and low current circuit

d] low voltage and low current circuit

4) In electropneumatic circuits,

a] spool is shifted by signal air

b] spool is shifted by control air

c] spool is shifted by electromotive force

d] all of the above

5) Why are electromechanical relays more popular than solid state relays?

a] they are reliable

b] less costly

c] both a] and b]

d] none of the above

6) In which control valve energy consumption reduces as load decreases?

a] conventional direction control valve

b] proportional direction control valve

c] both a] and b]

d] none of the above

7) Which of the following is a characteristic of servo valve?

a] open loop system

b] closed loop system

c] less contamination

d] all of the above

8) What is PLC?

a] Process logic control

b] Programmable language converter

c] Programmable logic control

d] Programmable logic converter

9) What causes burning of AC solenoid coil?

a] holding current

b] in rush current

c] current clamps

d] all of the above

10) When PLC connections are used instead of electrical connections, the order of operations to be performed can be interchanged by

a] changing hardwired connections

b] changing sequence of program

c] both a] and b]

d] none of the above

12) The heat generated in hydraulic systems can be absorbed by

a] lubrication

b] cooling

c] sealing

d] all of the above

14) For which of the following purpose hydraulic film acts as a seal between the machined cavity and spool?

a] to reduce leakage

b] for cooling purposes

c] for lubrication purposes

d] all of the above

16) Pressure applied on a fluid in a container is equally distributed in all directions and acts with

a] equal force on equal areas parallelly

b] equal force on different areas and at right angles

c] equal force on equal areas and at right angles

d] none of the above

17) Which law explains the behavior of hydraulic fluids under pressure?
a] Charles's law
b] Newtons law
c] Pascal's law
d] none of the above
18) Flow of oil in a pipe takes place due to
a] balanced forces
b] unbalanced forces
c] both balanced and unbalanced forces
d] none of the above
19) Pressure drop in pipes, occurs due to
a] frictional resistance
b] load
c] flow pattern
d] none of the above
20) How is laminar flow characterized in a straight pipe?
a] flow of high shear stress
b] flow of high velocity
c] flow of low-velocity
d] none of the above
21) Positive displacement pump used in hydraulic systems have
a] high viscosity of fluids
b] low efficiency
c] required volume of fluid cannot be discharged
d] all of the above
22) Electric motor has a speed of 1200 rpm and output rate of pump is 6 cc/rev] Calculate flow rate of pump in l/min
a] 6 l/min
b] 7]2 l/min
c] 5 l/min
d] none of the above
23) Calculate the power absorbed by the pump if, it has a flow rate of 20 cc/rev and develops a maximum pressure of 70 bar, when electric motor runs at a speed of 1200 rpm]
a] 1]9 kW
b] 2]8 kW
c] 2]3 kW
d] none of the above

24) Volumetric efficiency is the ratio of
a] theoretical flow rate to actual flow rate
b] actual flow rate to theoretical flow rate
c] actual fluid power to pump input power
d] none of the above

25) Which of the following is a hydrodynamic pump?
a] vane pump
b] centrifugal pump
c] gear pump
d] piston pump

26) What causes reduction in speed of the piston rod when the hydraulic cylinder is cushioned?
a] oil flow through small space
b] back pressure created in the system
c] both a] and b
d] none of the above

27) Which of the following is a hydraulic cylinder based on application?
a] welded
b] bolted
c] ram
d] all of the above

28) What happens when supply of oil to a single acting cylinder is stopped?
a] no pressure is exerted on the system
b] more pressure is exerted on the piston
c] less pressure is exerted on the piston
d] none of the above

29) When does expansion of spring and retraction of cylinder take place in spring type single acting cylinder?
a] oil pressure exerted is less than spring compression pressure
b] oil pressure exerted is more than spring compression pressure
c] oil pressure exerted and spring compression pressure are same
d] none of the above

31) In a telescopic cylinder, as the number of stages increase
a] diameter of piston rod also increases
b] diameter of piston rod decreases
c] diameter of the piston rod remains the same
d] none of the above

32) Why are bleed off circuits used?

a] bleed off circuit is used to restrict the flow of fluid into the hydraulic cylinder

b] bleed off circuit is used to restrict the flow of fluid out of the hydraulic cylinder

c] <u>bleed off circuits are used to reduce the speed of actuator</u>

d] all of the above

33) Which of the following is applicable for bleed off circuits?

a] bleed off circuits develop heat in the system

b] <u>bleed off circuits are used for resistive loads</u>

c] bleed off circuits are used for runaway loads

d] all of the above

34) What is the function of sequence valve used in hydraulic circuits?

a] <u>sequence valves are used to perform number of operations one after the other after the set pressure is reached</u>

b] sequence valves are used to perform number of operations continuously before the set pressure is reached

c] sequence valves after reaching set pressure oil is flown to the tank

d] all of the above

35) When is a pressure reducing valve used?

a] it is used when higher pressure than system pressure is required

b] <u>it is used when lower pressure than system pressure is required</u>

c] when absolutely zero pressure is required

d] all of the above

36) How is strong magnetic field in a solenoid achieved?

a] strong magnetic field in a solenoid is achieved, if coil acts as conductor

b] coil is surrounded by a iron frame

c] iron core is placed at the centre of the coil

d] <u>all of the above</u>

37) What is the DC range of of solenoids in pneumatic systems?

a] <u>12 V and 24 V</u>

b] 110 V and 220 V

c] both a] and b]

d] none of the above

38) Which of the following is used an output device on a ladder diagram?

a] proximity sensor

b] detent switch

c] <u>relay</u>

d] all of the above

39) The output device on a ladder diagram is represented by

a] square

b] circle

c] rectangle

d] semicircle

41) In mnemonics instructions, what does I in LDI indicate?

a] switch is normally open

b] switch is normally closed

c] it indicates operating of second switch

d] none of the above

42) In industrial applications hydraulic fluids have viscosity grade ranging from

a] 20 to 50

b] 70 to 95

c] 46 to 68

d] 15 to 44

43) High viscosity fluids have

a] low pressure drop

b] less power consumption

c] slow operation

d] all of the above

44) What is viscosity index?

a] effect of pressure on changes in viscosity

b] effect of temperature on changes in viscosity

c] effect of resistance between two surfaces

d] none of the above

46) Which property decides the behavior of fluid when mixed with water?

a] pour point

b] demulsibility

c] viscosity

d] oxidation

47) For any operation in a hydraulic system the fluid should have pour point

a] 20 0F below the lowest temperature

b] 20 0F above the lowest temperature

c] 20 0C below the lowest temperature

d] 20 0C above the lowest temperature

48) What is the disadvantage of petroleum based fluids?

a] low flash point

b] low density

c] light weight

d] all of the above

49) How is the water content in High Water Fluids (HFA) compared to oil content?

a] more oil than water

b] oil and water are in same proportion

c] more water than oil

d] contains only water

50) A fluid used in hydraulic systems should have

a] low oxidation resistance

b] high oxidation resistance

c] high oxidation enhancing ability

d] none of the above

1) At which pressure, petroleum oil used in hydraulic systems gets compressed by 1/2%?

a] 70 bar

b] 40 bar

c] 30 bar

d] 95 bar

2) What is the relation between temperature and specific weight for water glycol?

a] as temperature increases specific weight decreases

b] as temperature increases specific weight increases

c] temperature and specific weight vary linearly

d] none of the above

3) What is the relation between temperature and viscosity for hydraulic oil?

a] temperature and viscosity vary linearly

b] as temperature decreases viscosity decreases at atmospheric pressure

c] as temperature increases viscosity decreases at atmospheric pressure

d] none of the above

5) High Water Fluids contain

a] oil in water

b] water in oil

c] only water

d] none of the above

6) Viscosity of High Water Fluid is

a] greater than water

b] less than water

c] nearby water

d] none of the above

7) Adding an additive to water glycol fluids improves

a] flammability

b] viscosity

c] oxidation

d] all of the above

8) What is the characteristic of turbulent flow?

a] high velocity

b] the direction of flow and movement of particles is same

c] change in cross section does not affect the flow

d] all of the above

9) Which flow pattern gets affected when cross section of the pipe is changed?

a] laminar flow

b] turbulent flow

c] laminar and turbulent

d] none of the above

11) Speed of the actuator is affected by

a] cross-section area of the orifice

b] velocity of flow

c] pipe diameter

d] all of the above

13) In which of these applications Bernoulli's principle is widely used?

a] design of blowers

b] design of aircraft wings

c] design of propellers

d] all of the above

14) The total energy developed by the hydraulic oil in a system is given as

a] Total energy = (Potential energy + Pressure energy)

b] Total energy = (Potential energy + Kinetic energy)

c] Total energy = (Potential energy – Kinetic energy)

d] none of the above

15) If a pump gives higher flow rate to the valve then, pressure drop in the valve

a] increases

b] decreases

c] remains the same

d] none of the above

17) In Reynolds number (?vd) / µ, the letter µ denotes

a] kinematic viscosity

b] absolute viscosity

c] coefficient of friction

d] none of the above

18) The ratio of inertia force to viscosity is known as

a] Biot number

b] Reynold number

c] Cauchy number

d] Euler number

19) The Reynolds number for laminar flow is

a] more than 2800

b] more than 2000

c] less than 2000

d] between 2000 and 2800]

20) A pipe has a diameter of 0]2 m in which a fluid flows with a velocity of 0]3 m3/s] Determine whether the flow is laminar or turbulent calculating the Reynolds number] Assume kinematic viscosity = 0]5 × 10-4 m2 /s]

a] the flow is laminar having Reynolds number 1200

b] the flow is turbulent having Reynolds number 2100

c] the flow is laminar having Reynolds number 2200

d] the flow is neither laminar nor turbulent

21) What is the advantage of internal gear pump?

a] moderate speed

b] medium pressure

c] high viscosity fluids can be used

d] all of the above

22) The rotation of which inner element causes the liquid to pump out in centrifugal pumps?

a] internal gear

b] rotation of the impeller
c] cylinder rotor
d] none of the above
23) Which force causes vanes to come out of the rotor slots?
a] centripetal force
b] centrifugal force
c] friction force
d] none of the above
24) Which of the following statements is true?
a] combination of stator with rotor is known as cartridge unit
b] combination of stator with vanes is known as cartridge unit
c] combination of rotor with vanes is known as cartridge unit
d] none of the above
25) What is the advantage of flexible vane pump?
a] they can handle solids which are of large size
b] they can create good vacuum
c] both a] and b]
d] none of the above
26) Cartridge kits generate pumping chambers of various sizes, which
a] increase the flow rate
b] decrease the flow rate
c] increase and decrease the flow rate
d] none of the above
27) Which of the following statements is false for vane pumps?
a] wear in contact surfaces occurs due to continuous contact between vane tips and the cam ring
b] different sizes of cartridge kits can be replaced in same vane pump
c] elliptical cam ring is replaced by round cam ring to reduce unbalanced forces
d] none of the above
28) Balanced vane pumps are designed to have
a] fixed displacement
b] variable displacement
c] both fixed and variable displacement
d] none of the above
29) Cam ring of unbalanced vane pump is
a] round
b] elliptical

c] both a] and b]
d] none of the above
32) Which type of displacement is observed in gear pumps?
a] only variable displacement
b] only fixed displacement
c] both fixed and variable displacement
d] none of the above
33) What is the principle of operation used in gear pumps?
a] two gears rotate in same direction
b] two gears rotate in opposite direction
c] both a] and b]
d] none of the above
34) What causes suction of fluid into the gear pump?
a] when pressure drops during disengagement of teeth at the suction side
b] when pressure increases during disengagement of teeth at the suction side
c] when pressure drops during engagement of teeth at the suction side
d] when pressure increases during engagement of teeth at the suction side
35) How is the smooth and continuous discharge of fluid achieved in a gear pump?
a] increasing number of teeth
b] decreasing number of teeth
c] none of the above
d] all of above
37) The rotation of gears in internal gear pump takes place in
a] same direction
b] different direction
c] none of the above
d] all of above
38) How does the fluid flow in internal gear pump?
a] fluid enters the suction side between rotor, which is a large exterior gear and idler which is a small interior gear
b] fluid enters the suction side between rotor, which is a small exterior gear and idler which is a large interior gear
c] fluid enters the suction side between rotor and idler which rotate in different directions

d] none of the above

39) What causes internal leakage in internal gear pump?

a] less tolerance level between the meshing surfaces

b] more tolerance level between the meshing surfaces

c] no tolerance between the meshing surfaces

d] none of the above

40) What is the relation between pressure and overall efficiency for a gear pump?

a] as pressure increases, overall efficiency decreases

b] as pressure increases, overall efficiency increases

c] overall efficiency is not affected by change in pressure

d] cannot say

41) Which of the following statements is true for standard hydraulic cylinder and a telescopic cylinder?

a] telescopic and standard cylinders give same stroke length

b] telescopic cylinders give lesser stroke length than standard cylinder

c] telescopic cylinders give greater stroke length than standard cylinder

d] none of the above

43) Telescopic cylinders have

a] only two stage units

b] only three stage units

c] two or three stage units

d] multistage units

44) Which type of hydraulic cylinder has one piston connected to piston rod extended on both the sides of the cylinder?

a] telescopic cylinder

b] tandem cylinder

c] both a] and b]

d] none of the above

45) Which factor decides the working pressure of a hydraulic cylinder?

a] diameter of circular flange

b] bore diameter of cylinder

c] stroke length

d] all of the above

46) Which factor is considered while selecting the diameter of piston rod in hydraulic cylinder?

a] bore diameter

b] length of stroke

c] load

d] all of the above

47) Which end of the hydraulic cylinder, the male clevis is mounted on?

a] cap end

b] rod end

c] both a] and b]

d] none of the above

48) Which of the following is used for mounting purpose in hydraulic cylinders?

a] Female clevis

b] Circular flange

c] Trunnion

d] all of the above

49) How does cushioning affect the speed of the piston when the cylinder is cushioned at extreme end?

a] cushioning decreases the speed of piston near the extreme ends of the cylinder

b] cushioning increases the speed of piston near the extreme ends of the cylinder

c] cushioning increases the speed of piston at the beginning of the stroke in the cylinder

d] cushioning decreases the speed of piston at the beginning of the stroke in the cylinder

50) In adjustable type of cushioning,

a] piston rod can be moved at very slow speed

b] piston rod can be moved at increased speed

c] both a] and b]

d] none of the above

5) Which formula is used to calculate head loss in valves?

a] K2 (v / 2 g)

b] K (v / 2 g)

c] K (v2 / 2 g)

d] none of the above

6) What is the difference between vane pump and radial piston pump?

a] in radial piston pump, radial slots in vane pumps are replaced by radial bores which accommodate pistons

b] in radial piston pump, radial slots in vane pumps are replaced by radial bores which accommodate swash plate

c] in radial piston pump, radial slots in vane pumps are replaced by radial bores which accommodate both swash plate and pistons

d] none of the above

8) How many strokes does a single piston pump need to discharge oil?

a] one stroke

b] two strokes

c] three strokes

d] none of the above

9) How is the arrangement of pistons in piston pumps?

a] axially

b] radially

c] both a] and b]

d] none of the above

10) In which of these pumps, swash plate is used to translate the motion of rotating shaft into reciprocating motion?

a] radial piston pumps

b] axial piston pump

c] bent axis piston pump

d] all of the above

11) Which factors are considered while designing a axial piston pump?

a] use of swash plate

b] application in open loop or closed loop circuit

c] design of bent axis piston pump

d] all of the above

12) Angle of swash plate in axial piston pump is adjusted by

a] compensator

b] yoke

c] both a] and b]

d] none of the above

13) In axial piston pump, the yoke is pushed away from cylinder block due to which,

a] yoke angle increases

b] swash plate angle decreases

c] both a] and b]

d] none of the above

14) When the angle of swash plate decreases

a] flow rate increases

b] flow rate decreases

c] flow rate does not depend on swash plate angle

d] none of the above

15) What will be the discharge of oil in axial piston pump, when the angle of swash plate is zero?

a] discharge of oil is maximum

b] discharge of oil is minimum

c] there is no discharge of oil

d] none of the above

17) A bent axis piston pump has

a] pump axis bent

b] cylinder block which is inclined at an angle to the drive shaft

c] both a] and b]

d] none of the above

18) In which of these pumps, swash plate is replaced by cylinder block?

a] bent axis piston pump

b] radial piston pump

c] axial piston pump

d] none of the above

19) What happens when the distance between flange and cylinder block is varied?

a] piston displacement cannot be varied

b] variable flow rate of fluid can be achieved

c] fixed flow rate can be achieved

d] all of the above

20) What is the maximum angle between cylinder block and shaft axis?

a] 30o

b] 50o

c] 45o

d] all of the above

21) When does holding piston keep the angle between yoke and cylinder block maximum?

a] when set pressure is greater than load pressure

b] when set pressure is less than load pressure

c] when set pressure and load pressure are same

d] all of the above

22)

23) Low-torque high-speed motors are used in

a] cranes

b] winches
c] fans
d] all of the above

24) Which motor causes heavy loads due to its usage in order to move at constant lower speeds?
a] Low-torque high-speed motors
b] High-torque low-speed motors
c] both a] and b]
d] none of the above

25) Motors used in high speed applications have
a] high torque with high speed
b] low torque with high speed
c] high torque with low speed
d] none of the above

26) Which of the following is a type of low-torque high-speed motor?
a] radial piston motors
b] axial piston motors
c] bent axis motor
d] gear motor

27) Cam lobe hydraulic motor is a type of
a] axial hydraulic motor
b] orbit hydraulic motor
c] gear hydraulic motor
d] radial hydraulic motor

3] Vane type or Propeller type are which type of pump?
a) Piston pump
b) Centrifugal pump
c) High volume pump
d) Rotary pump

112] Which type of emergency shut off valve used in irrigation system?
A] Gate valve
B] Pressure release valve
C] Needle valve
D] Check valve

113] What is the purpose of irrigation valve?
A] Supply and control water flow
B] Maintain constant pressure
C] Reduce the water flow

D] Prevent fluid back flow

114] Why the discharge value is closed before stopping the centrifugal pump?

A] Prevent air lock

B] Prevent damage to check value

C] Prevent water hammering

D] Prevent damage to impeller

115] What must be the gap maintained from the bottom and sides during errection of centrifugal pump?

A] 50 cm

B] 60 cm

C] 80 cm

D] 85 cm

116] What is the purpose of diffuser vanes provided in the multi stage pumps?

A] Increase the working pressure

B] Provide uniform distribution of pressure

C] Decrease the working pressure

D] Regulate the fluid flow

117] What is the type of irrigation pump?

A] Single volute

B] Double volute

C] Rotary pump

D] Positive displacement pump

118] What is the result of loss of prime in centrifugal pump?

A] Pressure out put increased

B] Out let pressure decreased

C] Pump may damage

D] Pump produce poor delivery

119] What is the advantage of using centrifugal pump in irrigation?

A] Suction limit is more

B] Priming not required

C] Simple and economical

D] Over loading prevented

120] What is the name of centrifugal pump part?

A] Semi open type impeller

B] Open type impeller

C] Closed type impeller

D] Radial flow impeller

121] What is the typ of irrigation pump?

A] Rotary pump

B] Centrifugal pump

C] Vacuum pump

D] Hydraulic pump

www.ingramcontent.com/pod-product-compliance
Ingram Content Group UK Ltd.
Pitfield, Milton Keynes, MK11 3LW, UK
UKHW021912190726
13853UKWH00002B/636